Portrait of the ATLANTIC COAST EXPRESS

Stephen Austin

IAN ALLAN Publishing

Contents

First published 1997

ISBN 0 7110 2472 3

Published by Ian Allan Publishing

an imprint of Ian Allan Ltd, Terminal House, Station Approach, Shepperton, Surrey TW17 8AS. Printed by Ian Allan Printing Ltd, Coombelands House, Coombelands Lane, Addlestone, Weybridge, Surrey KT15 1HY.

Code: 9703/B2

Front cover: The down 'Atlantic Coast Express' hauled by 'Merchant Navy' class No 35019 *French Line CGT* at Basingstoke in March 1961. *B. Coates*

Previous page: The first version of the headboard, carried by No 35025 *Brocklebank Line* as she starts away under Howell Road from Exeter Central with an up 'ACE' in August 1952. *D. Cobbe/MNLPS Collection*

Back cover top: At Padstow, 'West Country' class No 34036 *Westward Ho* stands ready to depart with the up 'ACE'. *Colour-Rail*

Back cover bottom: 'West Country No 34017 *Ilfracombe* at Tavistock sometime in the mid-1950s. *R. E Vincent*

Below: The tower of the Palace of Westminster appears dwarfed by modern office blocks in this view from Vauxhall station; unfortunately, the clock tower is exactly in line with a nearer factory chimney. The 'MN' class engine is No 35025 *Brocklebank Line*, the coach is Corridor Third No 57 of set 838. *R.L. Sewell*

Preface: Riding to the West

by David Elliot

A jingle of cutlery, a clinking of glasses — not the first things that come to mind when one thinks of a speeding train; but my first memory of the 'Atlantic Coast Express' is of just those sounds when I walked through the corridor connection into the dining car, as it whirled through Sherborne at 70mph on its way from Salisbury to Exeter. A friendly sound, and a friendly train that brings back North Cornwall holidays in the 1930s. One of its pleasures was the three course lunch served at a mile a minute, notable for the virtuosity of the stewards pouring coffee and milk from two pots held well above the cup, and never spilling a drop.

Waterloo to Salisbury was then 'Lord Nelson' territory, and I would trek along the Waterloo platform to watch a handsome 'Nelson' from Nine Elms back onto the train. Surely this was the best-looking 4-6-0 on British rails? I thought it was, and never mind the 'Kings' and 'Castles' I might see later at Exeter St David's. A whistle; a shove from an 'M7' tank on the rear, and we were off down the South Western main line, eight tracks wide and level. I would look out for the massive Wimbledon flyover, new in the 1930s, and the second flyover at Worting Junction, where the four tracks divided into two for Southampton and two for Salisbury. We might be doing 80 when we passed Worting.

Salisbury to Exeter meant lunch in the dining car, and a switch-back ride behind an 'Arthur'. My father, then Assistant Traffic Manager of the Southern, had earlier persuaded the company to give Maunsell's 'N15' 4-6-0s names from Malory's *Morte d'Arthur*. He told me how at one naming session he had proposed *Joyous Gard* for one of the class, and the ASLEF man present had chipped in indignantly, 'What about the drivers, then?'. After lunch, I would break the rules and put my head out of the window to watch the 'Arthur' tackling the 1 in 80 of Honiton Bank; speed could be down to 15mph at the top and I remember the lazy click of the catch-points as the bogies rode over them. Then into the tunnel, and the downhill dash through Honiton into Exeter Central, where, with luck, I might spot a 'Z' class tank, one of the few eight-coupled engines to be seen on Southern metals.

'Arthurs' were too heavy to work west of Exeter, so the chunky 'U' and 'N' Moguls and the graceful 'T9' 4-4-0s ruled the rails to Okehampton, Bude and Padstow. The careful passage through Exeter St David's and the short journey to Cowley Bridge Junction gave a chance to see a Great Western express make its lordly way through to Plymouth or Paddington; the Southern, I felt, was definitely the poor relation at St David's. The 'ACE', probably now double-headed, would negotiate the sweeping curves before Okehampton (where a tea hamper would be handed in) and run slowly over the Meldon

Below: Seen from Normandy Way bridge, 'N' class No 31842 with the Sunday 12.6pm Plymouth–Exeter on 2 April 1961 accelerates under the land spans of the Royal Albert Bridge. Beyond is one of the towers of the road suspension bridge — the future in the making. *J.C. Beckett*

Viaduct, another place to lean out and look down into the canyon through which ran the little West Okement River.

Meldon Junction signalled the start of the slow but delightful run over the single-track North Cornwall line, one of the few which ran over hills rather than through them, as its builders did not have the money for bold engineering works. The names of the stations had a Will Hay ring to them — Otterham, Tresmeer, Egloskerry, St Kew Highway. In the summer there would be numerous 'meets', as the Americans call them, with up trains, to the accompaniment of tablet changing and bell ringing from those squat South Western signalboxes, which looked rather like greenhouses with their slate roofs that barely overlapped the windows. After a long day in the train would come the run along the Camel estuary and over the three-span truss bridge into Padstow, where Mr Penwarden the stationmaster would be on parade to usher us into a large hire-car for the last few miles to Trevone Bay, our holiday destination.

The end of the holiday was always a let-down, but the up journey offered one consolation prize — the ascent of the 1 in 37 bank from Exeter St David's to Exeter Central, as steep as the Lickey Incline and on a sharp curve with a tunnel at the top. It was exciting to feel the bankers clunk onto the rear of the train, hear the 'crow' whistling and feel the tilt as the train attacked the incline, which started just beyond the platform end. And when I leaned out on the up side, as I always did, I could enjoy the noble sight of four locomotives working all out to lift 12 coaches up the gradient — maybe an 'N' and a 'T9' on the head end, and at the rear a pair of 0-6-2 tanks giving it all they had, four columns of smoke laying a pall over the cathedral city. Steam in all its glory, and I count myself lucky to have known it.

David Elliot
January 1997

Above: No 34036 *Westward Ho* passing Exmouth Junction on 20 July 1962. The train is formed with BR Standard coaches, put into a set and given a number in the Southern style. The locomotive depot is in the background, and immediately above the train is a coal wagon on the hoist of the coaling plant.
F.W. Paige/MNLPS Collection

Author's Note

This impression of the 'Atlantic Coast Express' is more of an outline than a full specification, otherwise the shape of the thing would have been lost in an endless complexity of details. It also has a bias towards viewing the down workings; as a native of the south-east I could not avoid it, for if one is visiting the West Country, the run down is always more exciting than the return.

It is not always clear what the 'ACE' actually was. The public timetables were often vague, the Plymouth portion in particular not showing the name at all in many years. Tracing the schedule through the working timetables involved picking fragments out of four separate books, and the Working Timetable never quoted train names.

When, in summer, the various portions ran as complete trains (some advertised with the name and some not) and unadvertised reliefs could be put on, matters become more confused, leading some commentators to say that anything heading west from Waterloo in the mid-morning was an 'Atlantic Coast Express'. This was not the case, and the greatest number of 'ACEs' on a summer Saturday in the halcyon days of the late 1930s was five.

Further difficulties arise in asking what was or was not a through train. For instance, the up coaches from Seaton and Lyme Regis were attached to the 11.12am Exeter–Salisbury stopping train, which comprised the coaches which had formed the 9am from Torrington. The former are usually regarded as part of the 'ACE' but the latter are not. In tracing these interlocking operations some writers end up trying to describe the entire service, tying themselves and their readers in knots in the process. I have limited the number and length of strands in order to try and keep to the part of the pattern legitimately within our title.

The timetable and operating information comes from original documents held by the Public Record Office. The source books opened most frequently were the histories of the later LSWR engines and the Bulleid Pacifics by D.L. Bradley, and of the coaches by David Gould. There are excellent route books produced by both the Middleton Press and the Oakwood Press. Other sources include *The Locomotives of the Southern Railway* by W.G. Tilling, *Plymouth, A New History* by Crispin Gill, *The North Devon Line* by John Nicholas, *King Arthur Country in Cornwall* by Brenda Duxbury & Michael Williams, and the Sixth and Seventh Series Ordnance Survey Maps. The contemporary reports in the *Railway Magazine* are vital. Above all, the books by David Wroe on the Bude and North Cornwall Railways are so comprehensive that there can surely be little left to say about them.

I would like to thank the staff of the Public Libraries of Plymouth, Newton Abbot and Barnstaple; Alan Wilkinson of the Bideford & Instow Railway Group; Ted Crawforth, locomotive expert; Tim Robbins, carriage consultant; the Bluebell Railway; Terry Gough; Ron Sewell; John Duncan Gomersall; Brian Coates; the *Journal* of the Merchant Navy Locomotive Preservation Society, from whose archive I was able to draw; David Elliot, whose father Sir John Elliot started it all; Russell Pollinger of the Launceston Railway Circle; Richard and Toddie Irving; Nigel and Kay Bowman of the Launceston Steam Railway; Chris Austin; and my sister Janet Price who has kept me on the rails. I would also like to set down a general acknowledgement to the friendly people met while exploring the routes and stations.

Everyone wants to be associated with a famous train; there have been all sorts of apparitions in unlikely places, purporting to perpetuate the 'ACE', and the writer admits to being mixed up in several of them. Valiant efforts are being made at various locations on and off the route to restore what is left of the old railway, or even to reconstruct some of it. I hope you will support them by visiting — in particular — the groups working at Yeovil Junction, Barnstaple Town, Instow, Bideford, Launceston, Bere Ferrers, Bodmin (old rivals are friends now), and the Bluebell and Swanage railways. The relevance of these to the history of the train may be dismissed by purists, but it is a case of doing what we can to keep a great tradition going, and this must always be worth while.

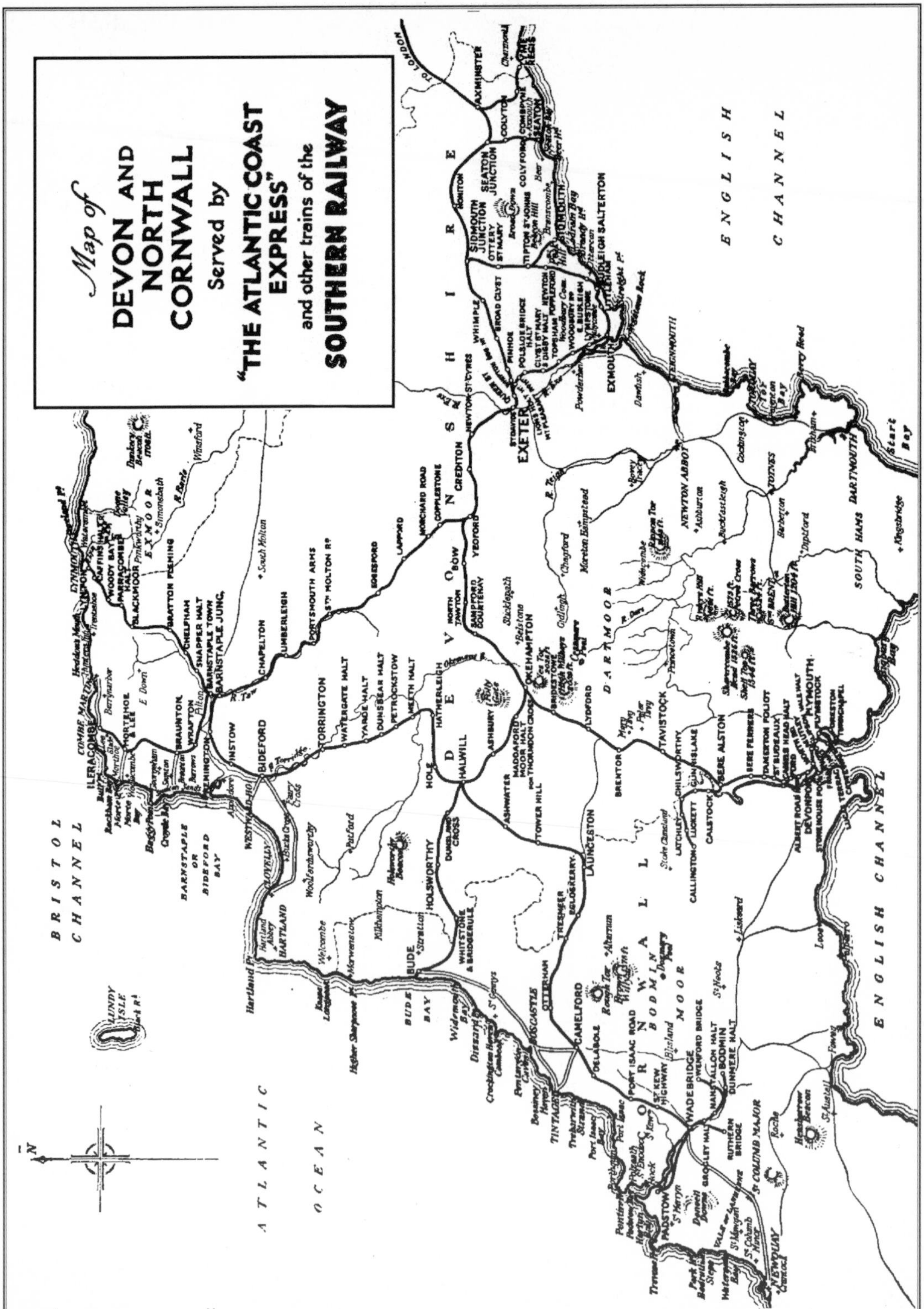
Map of
DEVON AND
NORTH
CORNWALL
Served by
"THE ATLANTIC COAST
EXPRESS"
and other trains of the
SOUTHERN RAILWAY
BRISTOL CHANNEL
ATLANTIC OCEAN
ENGLISH CHANNEL
DEVONSHIRE
CORNWALL
DARTMOOR
BODMIN MOOR
EXETER
PLYMOUTH
ILFRACOMBE
BARNSTAPLE
BIDEFORD
TORRINGTON
OKEHAMPTON
LAUNCESTON
BUDE
PADSTOW
WADEBRIDGE
BODMIN
TAVISTOCK
EXMOUTH
SEATON
SIDMOUTH
LYME REGIS
AXMINSTER
CREDITON
HOLSWORTHY
CAMELFORD
TINTAGEL
NEWQUAY
DARTMOUTH
LUNDY ISLE

Introduction

London's Waterloo station has been chiefly associated, throughout the mid-20th century, with the necessity of workaday travel. With County Hall, St Thomas's Hospital, the Palace of Westminster, New Scotland Yard, Whitehall and the Temple fanned out around it, it sat at the heart of the British Empire and was the staff entrance to what was, proportionately speaking, the greatest concentration of administrative power the world has ever known. Twice every day a human tide surged through Waterloo, in the service of that machine of government.

However, when the commuters had dispersed, the station took on another theme, echoing the ebb and flow of more distant tides. The Atlantic Ocean beckoned, and on the huge wooden destination indicator facing the middle of the concourse the names of suburbs were replaced with those of West Country villages.

At about a quarter past ten an empty train, 13 coaches long, would ease into the platform, bringing to sooty, stuffy London a promise of another world in its name. At the same time, a modest three-coach train is heading upstream beside the River Tamar, passing beneath Brunel's Royal Albert Bridge; another is pulling up the Slade Valley with a view of the Gower coast at its back; a still more modest outfit drawn by a four-coupled tank engine is trundling over the rippling, tree-hung River Torridge; at Halwill Junction a two-coach set is backing unhurriedly up to another one, while a small group of people waits for it to draw into the platform; and at Exeter Central a restaurant car chef and attendant are busy stocking their pantry.

Shortly before three in the afternoon, passengers from that long train are alighting on the quiet platforms of North Tawton in sight of Dartmoor, or at Eggesford beside the River Taw where salmon leap; while the coaches from out of those deep country byways are joined together, behind the most modern express engine in the country, roaring along the four-track main line through Basingstoke at 80mph.

All these images belong to the 'Atlantic Coast Express'.

To describe the 'ACE' as the mid-morning train from Waterloo to the West of England is to understate it, for it was more than a train — it was a great institution. Firstly, instead of merely racing from one city to another, it was a direct link between London and a whole host of country towns and villages.

Secondly, for those interested in railways, it embraced the busiest railway in the world, with 1,238 trains a day, and a peaceful single-track route with four passenger and two goods trains a day.

Thirdly, it was not a train but a whole plethora of trains. Like a tree, its coaches branched out from the Waterloo-Exeter trunk route to travel to and from Ilfracombe, Torrington, Bude, Padstow, Plymouth, Exmouth, Sidmouth, Seaton and Lyme Regis. Shortly before midday every day there would be five trains called 'ACE' on the move, heading up towards London, then in mid-afternoon up to seven portions of what left London as one train would be making their separate ways down the branches. The excellence of planning and performance which achieved it was found throughout the railway service in the period under consideration, but this was the masterpiece.

Left: A Map of Devon and North Cornwall served by the ACE, this appeared in the Southern Railway publication *Devon and Cornish Days*.
Robert Antell Collection.

35015
5

34072

1

History

The Concept

Herbert Walker, General Manager of the Southern Railway in 1923, was not pleased to find that his great new company was regarded by the British Public as a joke, its punctuality and facilities lampooned in the press and by popular writers such as J.K. Jerome. It was not fair, of course. To take the old South Western, although Waterloo station fully deserved all the ridicule it got before World War 1, it had been expensively rebuilt into the best terminus in the country, and into it ran an electric train service of the most advanced kind, all of it constructed in the difficult years of the war and the subsequent slump. But once the BP gets its teeth into a joke it is not easily persuaded to let go, and Walker realised that engineering achievement was not enough; he needed a new persuader. His solution, an innovative one for the time, was to engage a Public Relations Assistant. The man he chose, John Elliot, had been a cavalryman during the War and was then a journalist, but seldom has a conversion been more profound. By the time Sir John Elliot retired as Chairman of the London Transport Board in 1959, he had probably done more good for the railways than any other 20th century manager.

One thing Elliot saw was the marked contrast apparent in the presentation of the West of England services of the Southern and the Great Western Railways. The two companies had once competed directly for the London–Plymouth business, but although the Southern had a slightly shorter route to Exeter, the commencement of non-stop running from Paddington to Plymouth and the jolt of the Salisbury tragedy in 1906 had effectively knocked it out. On the publicity front the GW had invented the 'Cornish Riviera' and had been blowing the publicity trumpet for all it was worth for 20 years, so Elliot looked around for some tune which he could blow, and found it at Tintagel Castle.

Tintagel is a small port on the north Cornish coast, blessed with a ruined castle which modern research suggests may have been built as a 12th-century tourist attraction, after Geoffrey of Monmouth used the place as the location for his story of King Arthur and his knights. Its exploitation for the present-day tourist trade stems largely from the work of the Rev R.B. Kinsman, Vicar from 1851 to 1891, who like many Victorians believed that a creative approach to history was good for the bank balance.

The detail that this dubious shrine was four miles from a remote outpost of the railway should not deter a good PR man, so Elliot put to the December 1924 Board meeting a proposal for the next batch of express passenger engines to carry names from Arthurian legend — another innovation for Waterloo, which had never before named engines. He also wanted a train name, but fortunately he did not select it from the same source. A competition was run in the Southern Railway's staff magazine, and 'Atlantic Coast Express' was credited to Guard F. Rowland of Woking. The latter had an interest in the concept, as he was about to move to Torrington, but sadly just six years later he became the only person to be killed on the North Devon & Cornwall Junction Railway, being knocked down while shunting.

On the face of it this looks like the most inapt train title ever devised, even among the rash of named trains which broke out in the 1950s. Of the 10 termini which the train served, only one

Above left: This photograph is from *The Times* newspaper, dated 1 July 1952, and the original caption reads: 'The Atlantic Coast Express, hauled by the Merchant Navy class locomotive *Rotterdam Lloyd Line*, approaching Hook at over 70mph yesterday. It is one of the trains on the Southern Region of British Railways that are being speeded up on the new summer schedules.' *Times Newspapers Ltd*

Left: On a Saturday morning, 1 July 1961, the driver of No 34072 *257 Squadron* watches as a crowd boards his train at Wadebridge. The engine is blowing-off heartily in readiness for tackling the long climb to Otterham with a maximum load. *Dr T. Gough*

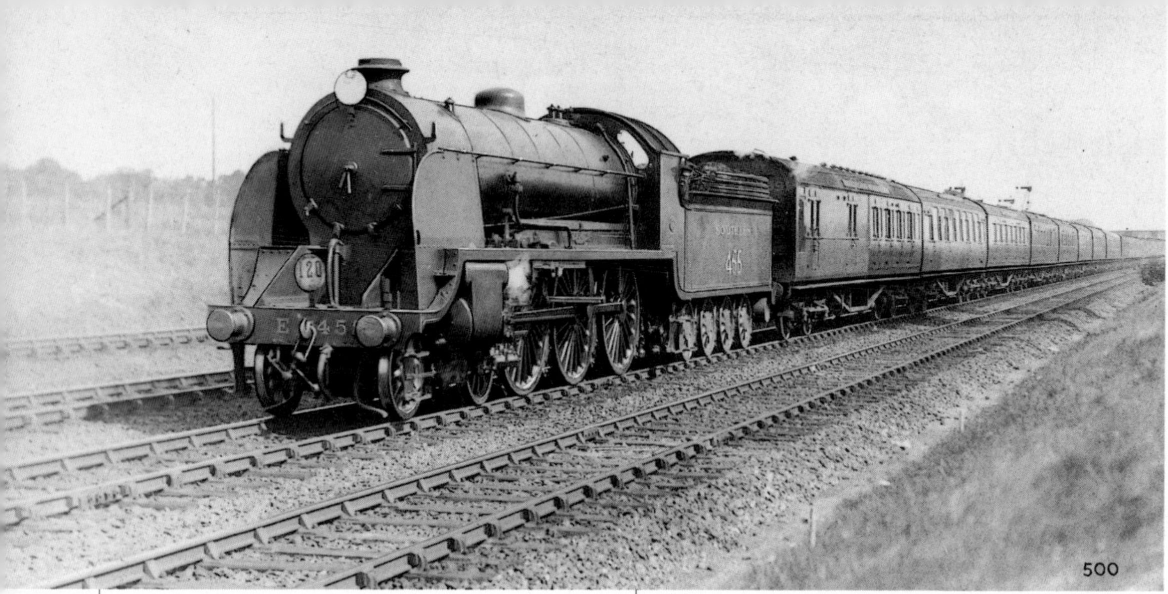

was actually on the Atlantic Coast, and with over half its mileage covered at speeds averaging around 30mph, station stops of up to 40min and a scheduled call at an unstaffed halt, to cynics it might hardly deserve to be called an express at all. However, it really was a most astute choice.

In England in 1925 ordinary folk did not feel a precise definition of the geography of their resort to be a prerequisite to the enjoyment of their holiday; they just wanted to know which train to board, and left the rest to the railway company. The 'Atlantic Coast' was just the image to attract them, and still is, and of course it ties in with the Tintagel connection. As regards the speed, 30mph is extremely fast where the only other conveyance is a pony and trap; and, for that matter, even with a late 20th-century motor car a traveller could not improve on the train's journey times, unless he was utterly reckless and selfish. There is also the point of view of the people in North Devon and Cornwall, then one of the poorest parts of the country. To them, this train of two or three coaches moving from station to station was not to be taken lightly, or for granted; it joined them to the rest of the world, and 'ACE' was a designation that suited them all.

This excellent research fell rather flat when the time came to apply it. There was no new train, either in the hardware sense or as a service; on the commencement of the 1926 summer timetable, the title was applied to the existing mid-morning West of England services.

The 11am down on Monday 19 July 1926 was seen off ceremonially from Waterloo behind engine No 779 *Sir Colgrevance*, but the rest of the service carried on as usual. Even this inauguration was delayed a week by what modern history calls the 'General Strike' but was referred to then as the 'Coal Stoppage'. There was no general publicity; the West Country press ignored it, though they reported the resumption of full services on the GWR and covered the death of George Flewellyn, the Inspector on *City of Truro* on her record run. In any event, the railways were completely upstaged by the weather, for on the previous Saturday a heatwave broke in terrific storms over the West. There were floods, a flock of sheep killed at Launceston, and 4½in diameter hailstones were picked up on Saunton Sands the next morning. With that and the opening of the Plymouth Carnival, a mere train was hardly newsworthy.

From then on matters improved somewhat; in August new coaches of Richard Maunsell's design began to appear, and with the new 'N' class 2-6-0s hauling it west of Exeter and the 'King Arthurs' east thereof — from 1928 a 'Lord Nelson' between London and Salisbury — the train could be regarded as something special.

The Southern Era

In that first summer of 1926 there were two 'ACEs' each way:

Down	M–S	11am	to Ilfracombe/Torrington/ Plymouth
	M–F	11.10am	to Padstow/Bude/Sidmouth/ Exmouth
	SO	10.25am	to Padstow/Bude
Up	M–S	10.22am	Ilfracombe/10.25 Torrington/ 10.15 Plymouth
	M–F	8.35am	Padstow/9.45 Bude/ 11.15 Sidmouth/10.40 Exmouth
	SO	10am	Padstow/11am Bude

Note — on all tables, traditional timetable abbreviations are used;
ie M-F — Mondays to Fridays;
SO — Saturdays only; Su — Sundays.

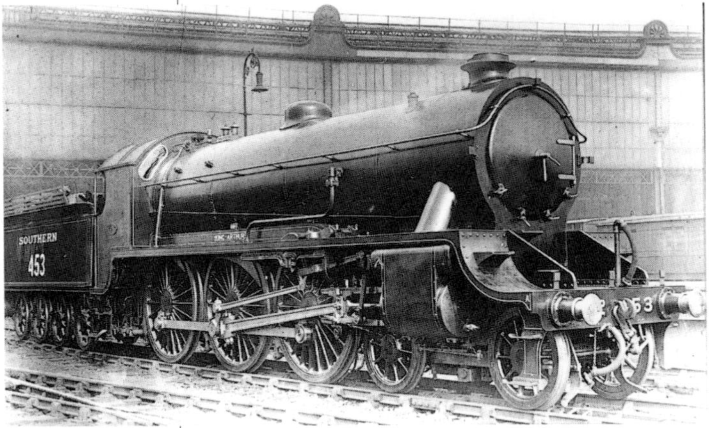

Above left: The 'ACE' of the 1930s; passing Worting Junction and approaching Battledown, where the outer tracks diverge to Bournemouth. This is thought to be the 10.38am to Ilfracombe. The engine is No 455 *Sir Launcelot*; the 12-coach train is led by Set No 391 in its summer formation of six coaches. *Real Photographs*

Above: 'LN' No 860 *Lord Hawke*, built in 1929, in Deepcut on a down train. The coaches are hardly a fit complement to the engine. *M.W. Earley*

Centre right: The first Maunsell 'N15' class engine, No 453, with the *King Arthur* nameplates, was shown to the Press at Waterloo in February 1925. The positioning of the plates was a mistake; they were far too inconspicuous. *W.J. Reynolds/Ian Allan Library*

Right: During the war amateur photography, while not totally proscribed, virtually ceased, and no one watched trains for fun, so this view is a rarity. No 21C8 *Orient Line* is passing Surbiton in September 1942, probably with the 10.50am down. *Dr T.F. Budden*

The Plymouth portion was detached and attached at Exeter Central; the Torrington portion at Barnstaple Junction. The Padstow and Bude portions divided and joined at Halwill Junction. The Sidmouth and Exmouth coaches left, and joined, the main train at Yeovil Junction and travelled on the rear of a local train which stopped at Axminster, Seaton Junction and Honiton. At Sidmouth Junction the Sidmouth coach was put on a branch line train which left at 3.7pm and the Exmouth coach was put on another train which left at 3.17pm. In the up direction the trains conveying these two coaches were combined at Tipton St John's.

There were of course other West of England services; for instance, on Saturdays the down Plymouth portion often ran separately from Waterloo at 11.4am, and Sidmouth and Exmouth had separate complete trains, but these were not 'ACEs' and are outside our scope.

The 'ACEs' were among a special group of trains whose guards' journals had to be sent in daily to the Divisional Operating Superintendents and to the Chief Operating Superintendent at Waterloo. These journals included the numbers of passengers carried. Further indication of their importance was the issue of load limits between Waterloo and Exeter: 11 bogie vehicles for the 11am, 13 for the 11.10 and 12 for the up trains. A loaded 12-coach train would weigh about 410 tons.

It is important to remember that the summer timetable applied only to some 10 or 12 weeks from early July to late September or early October, and the winter timetable covered all the rest of the year. When the winter timetable began, there was one train:

Down	M–S	11am to Ilfracombe/ Torrington/Plymouth/ Padstow/Bude
Up	M–S	10.22am Ilfracombe/ 10.25 Torrington/ 10.15 Plymouth/ 8.35 Padstow/9.45 Bude/ 12.15 Sidmouth/11.45 Exmouth

The Sidmouth and Exmouth coaches were attached to the main train at Sidmouth Junction. Here we see the multi-portioned nature of the 'ACE' which was claimed to be a record, although in fact it was second to the night newspaper train from Waterloo, which ran faster than the 'ACE' and conveyed vans with 11 different final destinations.

This set the pattern for the future, although in summer there was a lot of tinkering with the details. In the 1927 summer service, Lyme Regis and Seaton coaches were added to the 11.10am down and the up Padstow/Bude. They travelled on the same local train as the Sidmouth and Exmouth coaches. The timetable planners never seemed to make up their minds about Seaton and Lyme which drifted in and out of the service from year to year.

An alteration established by the second winter was to take the East Devon coaches off at Salisbury and attach them to the following down train. This began the association with the 12.38pm Salisbury–Exeter (later the 12.46 and after World War 2 the 12.36) and with the 11.12am Exeter–Salisbury, which brought the up coaches and arrived at Salisbury 9min before the 'ACE' proper. As the Ilfracombe portion also included one or more through coaches for Brighton, there was a lot of very slick shunting done at Salisbury, and it was to ease this that on a few up trains the engine was run through from Exeter to Waterloo, thus eliminating two light engine movements through the congested four tracks in Salisbury station.

At some time between 1929 and 1934 another portion was added, in the form of a coach which was taken off at Salisbury and attached to the 12.38 with the others, but ran right through to Exeter. This continued until the end of the service. Also in this period, the Sidmouth/ Exmouth service was changed to leave Sidmouth Junction as one train and divide at Tipton St John's.

An item which was dropped after the first couple of years on the weekday service, although it continued on Sundays, was a stop made by the 11.10 down at Surbiton to pick up passengers. This idea of a stop at a station on the edge of the London area was considered again by British Railways in 1949, but they did not think it worth while on this route.

On the subject of Sunday, here again Head Office did not appear to be able to make up its mind. There was always a train serving Plymouth, Ilfracombe and Torrington, resembling the basic winter weekday service; indeed, it was slightly faster than the latter. It never carried Bude or Padstow portions, and the North Cornwall line did not open at all on Sundays. This train at first had no official name but by 1933 it was billed as an 'ACE', and by the end of the decade it too was being run in two parts east of Exeter.

In the 1929 summer service the 11.10am down was changed to 10.41 and subsequently to 10.35, so that the Monday–Friday trains more resembled the Saturdays.

In 1926 there was very little difference in the service between Saturday and the other weekdays. As the country climbed out of the Depression, that changed and the Saturday rush became an institution. By the summer of 1937 there were five down Saturday 'ACEs': 10.35am to Ilfracombe, 10.38 to Ilfracombe, 10.41 to Padstow, 11.0 to Plymouth/Bude/Torrington and 11.6 to

Above: No 451 *Sir Lamorak*, with a clear fire and a full head of steam, climbing Honiton Bank on a prewar summer day with a down 'ACE'. *F.J. Arthur*

Torrington. There were four up: 10.10am Ilfracombe/8.40 Padstow/9.40 Bude, 10.30 Ilfracombe/10.22 Torrington, 10.35 Plymouth/10.40 Bude and 10.25 Padstow. The instructions limited the loads to 355 tons between Waterloo and Salisbury and 290 tons between Salisbury and Exeter, but these were not always observed, as accommodating the passengers was paramount.

The 1939 Saturday departures were 10.24am to Ilfracombe, 10.35 to Ilfracombe, 10.41 to Padstow, 10.54 to Bude and 11.0 to Bude/Padstow/Plymouth. The continuance of the relative decline of Plymouth is apparent and the public timetable tended to omit the name 'ACE' altogether from the Plymouth times.

The working of these peak services put everyone to the test: at Salisbury and Exeter, getting the engines changed and the train away before the next one was panting at the home signals; going all-out up Ilfracombe bank, an 'N' and an 'M7' on the front and another 'M7' on the rear; a pair of 'T9s' battling up past Higher Trethern with the Atlantic wind blowing straight up the firemen's dungarees; the tricky business of crossing trains that were longer than the loops. And remember that until October 1936 they were working Waterloo with mechanical signalling and nine boxes in five miles, the improvements at Exeter Queen Street were not completed until 1930, and they were sharing with the Great Western a cramped four-platform station at Plymouth North Road until enlargement in 1939.

At Padstow's tiny terminus the fish sidings had to be cleared on Friday to make room for the extra coaches. Ilfracombe was rebuilt with more sidings in 1928. At Bude the quay branch headshunt had to be used until 1939, when it was equipped with one carriage siding, all there was room for. At Waterloo on Saturday morning (then part of the working week for most offices), not only were there the electric trains, some 40 an hour each way, but every steam-hauled departure had an empty carriage stock (ECS) movement, a light engine and an outgoing carriage pilot to fit in. The timings for ECS and light engines were not specified in the Working Time Table, with the exception that paths were laid down for ECS movements from Clapham Yard to Waterloo. In 1927 these were, for mid-morning:

Clapham dep	*MFSO*				
	9.13	9.29	9.53	9.59	10.09
W'loo arr	9.25	9.41	10.4	10.13	10.21
Clapham dep	*SO*		*FSO*		
	10.13	10.18	10.24	10.29	10.43
W'loo arr	10.24	10.30	10.35	10.39	10.57

The 10.9 path was the one used all the year round by the 11.0 'ACE'. By 1932 it had become 10.10, and later when the departure time changed to 10.50 it became 10.2.

In the afternoon the emptied arrivals were sent out on the Windsor line, to go all the way down via Staines to Woking or Weybridge and up the main line to Oatlands, there to set back into the long sidings for stabling until the following weekend.

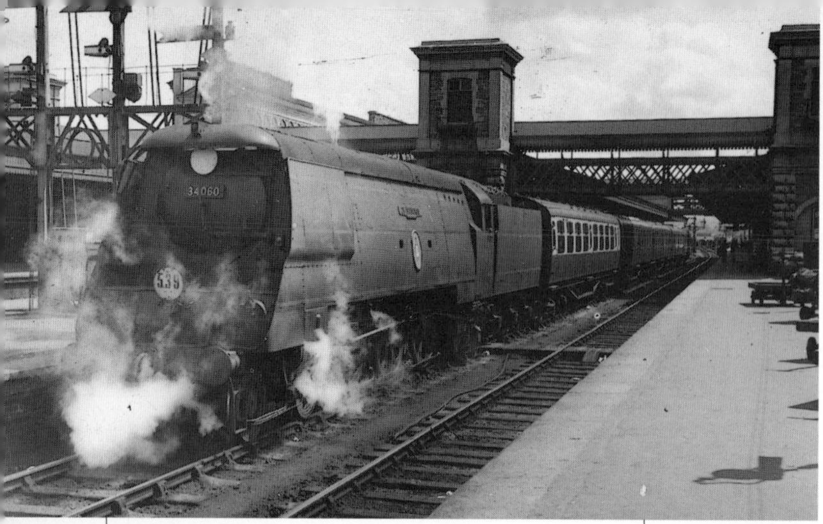

Left: A down train standing at the middle platform in Exeter St David's on 21 May 1951; engine No 34060 *25 Squadron*. The leading coach stands out in the new red and cream livery.
C.C. Pearson

Below left: On the evening of 24 August 1951, 'N' class No 31832 and an 'M7' lift another load of visitors up the bank to Mortehoe, just north of Heddon Mill.
Ian Allan Library

Left: The photographer is standing by Battledown flyover, and No 35021 *New Zealand Line* is on the Salisbury line, with the Bournemouth lines on each side. The first three coaches, Set No 963, were the first Bulleid coaches built. *B. Morrison*

Right: After the Salisbury engine change, No 30751 *Etarre* sets out for London. Note the driver with his pipe and handcloth. The air-operated and electrically-detected signal is another gem. *R.K. Evans*

Those summers of the late 1930s were halcyon days. But the Southern managers knew very well whence the increased spending power of their passengers was derived — rearmament; and the schedule for evacuation of the civilian population of Portsmouth, Gosport and Southampton had been in their files for two years. The winter timetable, due to commence on 25 September 1939, was printed as usual; but it was not used.

The National Emergency

On Wednesday 30 August 1939 the timetable was suspended and with it disappeared all train names and such frivolities. But although the 'ACE' name was not seen again until 6 October 1947, the train itself did not cease; it remained at the core of the service structure and was, if anything, more important in the context of the reduced wartime timetables.

For a couple of weeks the only morning West of England trains were the 9am from Waterloo and the up 8am Plymouth/7.55 Ilfracombe/7.55 Torrington. There was of course a massive traffic flow at this time, in the form of the evacuations, and with a lot of people revelling in their new authority not to tell anyone what was going on in the interests of 'security' and another lot striving to keep things going, a good time was had by all! They tried to resume the normal timetable on 18 September but that did not work, and a reduced *ad hoc* service ran from 16 October. After some high-pressure work in the offices, a new timetable was commenced on 20 November.

In this the down train left at 10.35am for Ilfracombe/Torrington/Plymouth/Padstow/Bude, the up train being 8.15am Ilfracombe/8.15 Torrington/8.20 Plymouth/8.22 Launceston/8.2 Bude. The schedules west of Exeter were virtually unchanged from those of peacetime. The main change was an addition of some 40min running time between Waterloo and Exeter, which proved rather too pessimistic, so a slight speed-up was made from 1 January 1940, in which the Exeter times remained the same but the Waterloo departure was put back to 10.50am and the arrival brought forward from 2.35pm to 2.25.

In May 1940 the North Cornwall through coaches were removed in favour of heavier loading on the Plymouth portion, which was now regularly at six coaches. However, as the prospect of invasion receded and it became clear that it was going to be a long war, 'business as usual' gained strength as a policy; apart from the movements of forces personnel, people continued to take holidays and many London workers were travelling down whenever they could to see their families, evacuated to the West Country. The Padstow, Bude, Exmouth and Sidmouth coaches

were back by the beginning of 1941, and the train began running in two parts again, the 10.50am followed by a 10.59 down and the up 12 noon off Exeter followed by a 12.15pm. The scheduled formations of these were: 10.50 down — two 3-sets Ilfracombe, two Corridor Thirds and one Brake Composite Torrington, Restaurant and one Brake Composite Exeter: 10.59 down; 2-set and one Corridor Third Plymouth, 2-set Padstow, Brake Composite Bude, Restaurant Exeter, Brake Composite Exmouth, Brake Composite Sidmouth, Brake Composite Exeter (attached to the 12.55pm Salisbury-Exeter). The up portions were divided between the first and second trains in the same way.

The restaurant services, which had been summarily stopped on 1 September 1939, were resumed on 16 October, after the Powers realised that folk must eat even when there was a war on; they were taken off again in June 1942 for all except a selected few trains. The 'ACE' retained its restaurants, running through to Ilfracombe and Padstow (Plymouth on Sundays) respectively, until the spring of 1944, when all train catering closed down. The vehicles were still running after then, for everything with seats was needed, but the kitchens were boarded up and the dining seats might well be occupied by German prisoners on their way to camps at Holsworthy, St Teath and Wadebridge. The rest of the train would be crowded with uniforms, for, besides the Navy at Plymouth, there was an experimental unit at Appledore, huge store depots at Launceston, Tower Hill, Halwill and Whitstone, airfields at St Eval, St Merryn, Davidstow and Chivenor, and an American Army hospital at Tavistock.

Traffic continued to grow, and from 4 May 1943 on Tuesdays, Wednesdays and Thursdays the 'ACE' was regularly loaded to 16 coaches between London and Salisbury and 14 between Salisbury and Exeter. Soon they were taking the 16 through to Exeter at weekends, and that was no joke. Fortunately, by then the 'Merchant Navy'

Above: This early 1950s view at Brookwood is probably the Saturday Ilfracombe train at speed. Locomotive No 35005 *Canadian Pacific* has a bracket on the smoke deflector plate for carrying the 'Devon Belle' emblem. This engine has been preserved in her rebuilt form. *R.F. Dearden*

class engines were available to haul them. Trains of that length extended out of Waterloo's platforms and blocked the entrance, so they had to be loaded in two parts, then joined up and sent off as quickly as possible; the yard foreman obtained permission from the signalman to start, then told the driver and showed him a yellow flag or lamp. In the up direction they were divided at Clapham Junction and the rear six coaches were brought up by one of the carriage shunters.

Work was disrupted by intensive and accurate enemy bombing. On 7 September 1940 the line was cut near Lambeth Bridge, and Waterloo was out of action until the 25th. Steam trains such as the 'ACE' terminated at Surbiton and later at Woking, with Raynes Park goods depot used as an engine stabling point. Further closures occurred on 15–17 October, 8–10 December and 29–30 December. During the second of these, some trains were sent to Victoria, which seems to have been tolerable, for in 1942 a contingency timetable was issued allowing both 'ACEs' to use Victoria, via Tulse Hill and Herne Hill or via Balham. They would have crossed from the up through to the up Sutton line at Wimbledon C Box, and from the down Haydons Road to the down through at Wimbledon A. Following the night of 16 April 1941, when Waterloo and Nine Elms engine shed were hit, steam trains were terminated at Clapham Junction until 26 May.

While Waterloo to Woking was known as 'Bomb Alley', the West Country did not go unscathed. Any port or railway station was at risk; even Padstow was hit in October 1940. On 21 March 1941 Plymouth was attacked, two trains being hit and burnt out, and in the following month the city centre suffered more complete devastation than any other in Britain. All the stations were damaged, the railways were cut, and traffic to Cornwall was maintained over the Southern's North Cornwall line with reversals at Wadebridge, Bodmin and Bodmin Road. Exeter was also heavily bombed during the middle period of the war.

When an 'Air Raid Warning Red' was on, trains were restricted to 25mph in daylight and 15mph in darkness, and stopped at the first station to allow passengers to leave if they wished. Those who remained had to close the windows, pull down the blinds and sit on the floor. Meanwhile the driver was proceeding with caution, prepared to stop short of any obstruction.

The rain of German bombs on the long-suffering railwaymen was matched by the deluge of paper from the Head Office at Deepdene House. From a notice from the General Manager instructing senior persons 'to be alert and confident, check and rebuke loose opinion, and remove officials who spread alarm or despondency', to details of the liaison tasks of the War Department Railway Construction Engineer based at Salisbury, all was laid down in print. In the event of invasion, the men were instructed to keep the railway running until receiving the order 'PACKET', which was to evacuate all engines and to block lines by demolishing selected overbridges. On the West of England line these were the A338 bridge east of Salisbury and the A30 west of it.

By 1942 two complete contingency timetables existed, both built round the 'ACE'. 'P.X.' was similar to the Sunday service and had a down 11am to Plymouth (arr 5.12pm)/Ilfracombe (5.26)/Torrington (5.20) and an up 10am Plymouth/9.50 Ilfracombe/10.2 Bideford reaching Waterloo at 4.10. Connection was made at Okehampton with a 4.20pm to Padstow (6.39)/Bude (5.23) and an up 8.30 Padstow/9.48 Bude. 'P.Y.' was a reduced version, in which the train stopped at all stations and the overall journey would have taken about 1½hr longer. These would have been put into operation on issue of the code from the Divisional Superintendent's Office, evacuated to Woking. There was another code — 'P.Z.' — all passenger trains stopped.

These emergency schedules and the other grim orders were not invoked, but the reality was still grim enough. And through it all the trains kept rolling.

The British Railways Era

Within a matter of weeks of the end of the war in Europe, the Southern made a strong bid to resume the progress of the 1930s where it had left off. This was just what would be expected from the dynamic team of Eustace Missenden as General Manager, John Elliot now as Deputy General Manager and Oliver Bulleid as Chief Mechanical Engineer. A revolutionary shape appeared in the form of the 'West Country' class engines — able to haul a full-length train through Exeter to the West of England routes, where they gave in one jump a 40% increase in power over the 'N' class. In October 1945 a new coach was presented to the public: a longer, more spacious vehicle in which the traditional compartment doors were replaced by wide picture windows. By the autumn of 1946 the new-look 'ACE' was established.

At first the service remained the same, with the 16-coach train slogging down to Exeter. A new timetable came out for 1 May 1946, showing the train serving Ilfracombe, Torrington, Padstow, Bude and Plymouth on weekdays and two trains, a Padstow/Bude and an Ilfracombe/Torrington, on Saturdays. The holiday traffic came back, but not as strongly as hoped, for in the spring of 1949, after four years of peace, it was revealed that numbers of passenger engines, including 'King Arthurs' and new 'West Countries', were parked out of use at main depots.

The restaurant cars were brought back into use on 1 October 1945, but for some years, with food shortages and rationing, the service was maintained with great difficulty. The Emett cartoon of the chef grabbing a rabbit from a lineside field was not all that far-fetched a fantasy. Not only food was short, but also coal and just about everything else. Passengers rode chilly and dirty, for steam heat stayed firmly off and it was not until 1952 that soap and towels were available in the lavatories. Just to add to the gloom, fares, which had shot up during the war, continued to rise — a phenomenon unknown before the war.

1947 started with an extremely harsh winter, one of the few when the lines in the West Country were blocked by snow. The high, exposed sections from Okehampton to Halwill and Tavistock were the most vulnerable, and on at least one day the up Padstow/Bude 'ACE' was turned back at Halwill onto the North Devon & Cornwall Junction line to Torrington.

The winter coal crisis, which started in 1947 when surface stacks were iced up and immovable, became an annual event, until in 1951 it did what the war had failed to do: stopped the 'ACE' altogether. It was suspended from 12 February until 2 April, and all on-train catering was also cancelled during this period. It was not surprising that the Southern Region was keen to bring its new diesel-electric locomotives into service. Incidentally, during its absence, South Molton Road station was renamed King's Nympton on 1 March.

All these upsets were of course blamed on Nationalisation and the British Transport Commission, and however unfair were the jibes, it was extremely tactless of the Railway Executive to make such an issue of choosing new colour schemes at a time when the passengers just wanted a reasonable train service and didn't give a damn what colour it was. The engines were painted black, to match the dirt which it was no longer economical to clean off, apart from the 'Merchant Navies' which were bright blue, and carmine & cream was applied to some of the Bulleid-designed coaches from new. By 1956 sanity and green paint were restored. (The writer is unrepentant about this, believing that the only place for red, white and blue on a train is on the flags on the front of the Bulleid Pacific heading the 'Golden Arrow'.)

At last, in the winter 1947 service, commencing on 6 October, the 'ACE' title was back — and so were the through coaches to Seaton, Exmouth and Sidmouth. The Seaton coach was conveyed to Seaton Junction by the 12.46pm Salisbury–Exeter and the other two were detached at Sidmouth Junction. However, Plymouth slid further down in status; it lost its up through portion and did not regain it until summer 1952. In the meantime it had to be content with a connection at Salisbury off the 10am to Brighton/Portsmouth. The up train, 8.25am Padstow/9.35 Bude/10.15 Ilfracombe/ 10.15 Torrington, had no East Devon portions either. Although the latter kept their through coaches by other services, the starting times necessary to meet the 'ACE' were presumably considered too late to be called a morning service and too early to allow visitors an extra half-day before leaving. This was a curious reversal of the prewar arrangement.

The 11am down departure was still there on Sundays, but it was not named and ran only to Plymouth, with good connections from Exeter to Ilfracombe/Torrington and Okehampton to Bude/Launceston. There was a Sunday 9.50am Ilfracombe/10.2 Bideford to Waterloo and a 10am Plymouth to Portsmouth/Waterloo. There was never again to be a named Sunday service.

For the 1949 summer a third Saturday train began running, down at 10.35am to Padstow/ Bude and up at 9.52am Padstow/10.58 Bude. The Saturday rush began to build up, chiefly because of the adoption of the five-day working week in factories and offices. Because the employment rate was also rising, once the change to a five-day week had started, most employers granted it within a couple of years. Other West of England trains were introduced during this period, reducing the pressure on the 'ACE' and offering the prospect of reduced train loads and improvements on the schedules, which were still largely unchanged from those of wartime. This was seen in the 1950 season, when a quarter-hour was knocked off the Waterloo–Exeter schedule.

Notwithstanding the apparent surplus of stock hitherto, by the spring of 1951 the Railway Executive claimed that there was such a freight traffic backlog, exacerbated by the coal crisis, that it could not release enough engines to work summer passenger services. The summer timetable, normally beginning in mid-June, was put back until 2 July, to end on 9 September.

The great year was 1952. The 11am departure time was restored and there was an 11.5 taking the Plymouth/Exmouth/Sidmouth/Seaton portions which ran on Mondays and Fridays 30 June–1 August, Mondays-Fridays 4–29 August, and Mondays,Fridays & as required 1–12 September. The up service was 10.30am Ilfracombe/10.30 Torrington/8.30 Padstow/9.30 Bude/9.50 Plymouth/11.40 Lyme Regis/12.42pm Yeovil Town, with a 9.40am Padstow/10.40 Bude following it up to Exeter and extended to Waterloo on the same dates listed above. The latter was very much faster, as it ran into Exeter only 28min after the main train which had started 1hr 10min earlier, accomplished by omitting stops.

On Saturdays there were now three down 'ACEs', 10.22am Padstow/Bude, 10.54 Ilfracombe/ Torrington and 11.0 Plymouth/Padstow/Bude; and five up, 8.30am Padstow/9.30 Bude,

10.30 Ilfracombe, 10.48 Torrington, 10.45 Padstow/11.45 Bude and an optional 11.45 Bude as a separate train. Plymouth, though back in the list for the up weekday train, had no up portion on summer Saturdays and never regained it.

At the same time, through engine working between Waterloo and Exeter became usual, and there was a substantial speed-up. Accelerations claimed were 13min to Sidmouth and Exmouth, 14min to Exeter, 12min to Ilfracombe and Torrington, 13min to Plymouth, 35min to Padstow and 39min to Bude. The up time was cut by no less than 38min from Exeter to Waterloo, the starting times being the same but the arrival time brought back from 4.18pm to 3.40. It was in this timetable that the 83min Waterloo–Salisbury booking appeared, the first 60mph start-to-stop schedule on the Southern, although it applied only on Mondays to Fridays and not until 1961 was the sacred 'mile a minute' obtained in the up direction.

This lively running was continued into the following winter, when the savings over the previous winter's times were 21min to Exmouth and Sidmouth, 24min to Ilfracombe, 34min to Torrington, 23min to Plymouth, 61min to Padstow and 48min to Bude, with the up acceleration again 38min. This was by any standards a tremendous advance, and showed that the Southern management was determined to use the excellence of its civil engineering and locomotives, and of course the expertise of its staff. It is only fair to remind steam enthusiasts

Above: This photograph is typical of the confusion that can arise. It is dated 10 August 1957, which was a Saturday, but is also marked 'Up "ACE" 3.40' which was the weekday time. It is probably the Ilfracombe train. The location is near Wimbledon.
MNLPS Collection

that these schedules were designed to exploit the diesel-electric locomotives, but when the latter departed, the men had no difficulty in maintaining the timings with steam.

It was no secret that the people in the firm next door were often struggling, but it was rare indeed for a Southern train to get out of kilter. It was at some time in this period that an up 'ACE' was going well on the final dash down from Milepost 31, approaching the built-up area, when the crew heard a thump from the front end of their 'Merchant Navy'. It was still running all right, so they carried on to Waterloo on time. There was, however, rather more steam drifting about than usual, so the driver had a look round after he stopped, and found that the front cover of the middle cylinder had completely vanished!

At this time, as before the war, the operating bible, the Working Time Table, did not specify the light engine movements in and out of Waterloo, but gave paths for incoming ECS movements:

	SO			
Clapham dep	9.45	10.2	10.5	10.19
Waterloo arr	9.54	10.11	10.14	10.28

Above: The River Axe at Axminster station. Starting away past the brush factory is the 4.35pm Exeter–Salisbury stopping train, hauled by 'N15' No 30450 *Sir Kay*. Behind the coaches is one of the West of England newspaper vans on its way back to London.
J.C. Beckett

Left: During 1950 Hurstbourne Viaduct was overhauled. On 24 November No 35013 *Blue Funnel* on the down 'ACE' eases past the workings, where the up line has been removed.
British Railways

The service remained in the same basic form through to 1963. The winter train was largely unchanged from year to year: down, 11am Ilfracombe/Torrington/Padstow/Bude/Plymouth/Exmouth/Sidmouth/Seaton, the Seaton coach going down to Seaton Junction on the 12.36pm Salisbury-Exeter; up, 10.30am Ilfracombe/10.30 Torrington/8.30 Padstow/9.30 Bude/9.45 Plymouth/12.42pm Yeovil Town. The Yeovil Town coach was brought round to Yeovil Junction, a 4min run, by the branch train (known locally as 'The Bunk'), then forward to Salisbury on the 11.12am from Exeter, which now all the year round was an extension of the 8.55am from Ilfracombe. The restaurant set worked to and from Exeter.

In summer the Plymouth/Padstow/Bude portions were run separately from Waterloo to Exeter in the 11.5am path, and from Exeter to Waterloo, starting at 12.18pm with the rest following at 12.30. The times west of Exeter were the same.

During the 1950s the holiday traffic built up to its all-time record in 1957. The summer Saturday scenes at Waterloo were quite remarkable, with that huge concourse proving none too big. Large tetrahedra marked with letters 'A' to 'E' were hung above it, and the destination board told passengers to queue under the letters for the different trains. Amazingly, this system worked well. The cab road was also used for queuing. Travellers were marshalled according to their destinations, and with luggage and children to manage, the vast majority of them probably did not know when their train actually started and could not have cared less whether it had a name on it or not. Out on the line, empty trains coming up from Clapham Yard ran on the up main through line to Loco Junction, where they were turned onto the down Windsor local. They stopped at Vauxhall station to embark the restaurant crews, then drew up nose to tail behind Signal WB211. A man posted there flagged them forward into the station as instructed by the signalbox.

Of the many departures, only three were 'ACEs': 10.35am Padstow/Bude, 11.0 Ilfracombe/Torrington, and 11.15 Plymouth/Padstow/Bude, and the latter was not, strictly speaking, billed as being an 'ACE', thus proving how confusing and devaluing is the idea of applying a name to more than one service on one day. There were then four up: 10.30am Ilfracombe, 10.48 Torrington, 11.0 Padstow and 11.45 Bude.

As before the war, the East Devon branches enjoyed separate through trains on summer Saturdays. After 1957 Seaton and Lyme Regis suffered a decline, in that they ceased to have their coaches brought down in the 'ACE', although they continued to enjoy other through services until the end of 1962. Apart from that, the following summers and winters were pretty much the same, 1963 being the last summer in which all the branches bloomed as they had done since 1899.

While everything seemed to the observers to be going splendidly, the men who had to operate the railway were encountering problems which presaged worse to come. The public did not think an old train still in service was splendid; they called it old-fashioned. They and the top management wanted big projects, preferably under the 'Modernisation' banner, and were less interested in keeping the existing set-up running. In theory, the electrification of the Kent lines released ample steam locomotives and coaches for use in the West and enabled the older stock to be discarded, but all such changes meant upheavals; organising spares, getting used to the wrinkles in repairing a different engine, becoming familiar with it so as to examine and oil it quickly in the dark without missing anything. Imagine yourself, a fitter at Exmouth Junction, used to dealing with the same bits and pieces of the 'N' class all your life, then along comes this thing called a 'U1' with an extra cylinder in the middle, where you have to squeeze yourself in to check cotters and the rest of it. Then, after a few months, someone decides they do not want it after all and the whole lot is changed around again. After the relative stability of the 1950s, the staff must have felt it was, as in the song, 'just one durned thing after another', and the 1960s came in with another bout of trouble from the weather.

The elements took charge during the autumn of 1960, when a series of rainstorms caused the worst flooding of the century across southern England. On 30 September the River Taw covered the track near North Tawton and the River Yeo did its bit around Crediton, demolishing bridge No 547 at Dunscombe near Newton St Cyres. The following night there were 30 slips and washouts on Honiton Bank alone, and a lot of the restoration work was washed away again on 6 October. The 'ACE' was run via Taunton and Westbury to Salisbury, but the vital Exeter-Crediton line was closed until a temporary bridge was completed after two weeks' continuous work in dreadful conditions. In January 1961 a slip at Hook, where the line runs on a hillside ledge, needed prolonged work and Sunday trains ran via Hounslow and Reading to Basingstoke. The severe winter of 1962–63 brought everything to a standstill west of Okehampton. Buckhorn Weston tunnel was blocked by snow on 27 December and on the afternoon of 3 January a blizzard caught the up 'ACE', which reached London 3½hr late. In August 1963 the boot was on the other foot, when flooding forced Western trains to use the Southern route between Yeovil and Exeter.

Throughout these years the civil engineers continued to improve the line, especially with a large signalling project completed in 1960. New

Left: The Torrington 'ACE' departing from Barnstaple Junction on 19 May 1959; a typical formation of a Maunsell Corridor Third and a Bulleid Brake Composite drawn by 'M7' No 30255. *K.L. Cook*

boxes were built at Sherborne, Crewkerne, Chard Junction, Honiton and Exmouth Junction, and equipment was updated at many locations including the North Cornwall line. The relining of Buckhorn Weston Tunnel was a major job, lasting on and off for over three years. This tunnel, like Honiton Tunnel, suffered chronically from ingress of water. For three periods, 9 March to 2 April 1958, 21 September 1958 to 27 May 1960 and 23 April to 14 May 1961, single line working was operated through the tunnel, the trains rumbling by at 15mph while the other road was used by the engineers to haul in, among other things, 1,600 tons of ballast to remake the floor. To control it a signalbox was erected at the east end, called Abbey Ford — not to be confused with an earlier box of the same name down near Buckhorn Weston village.

After all these developments, the few years from, roughly, 1958 to 1962 saw the 'ACE' reach its zenith. The magnificent Rebuilt Bulleid Pacifics swished up and down the main line, while at the outer extremities 60-year-old Drummond tanks buffered up to the coaches as they had done for donkey's years. Passengers sat and passed the time during the shunting at Okehampton, with a view out across to Exmoor, or at Halwill, with nothing to see but a grass cutting side. Southern ramblers alighted at Brentor or Port Isaac Road where there was not another house in sight, while their bicycles might share the van with a calf trussed up in a sack, or a crate of chickens. On the journey, enthusiasts could look out for the '0415' class Adams 4-4-2T engine at Axminster on 'Lyme Billy', an '0298' class Beattie 2-4-0T pottering about Wadebridge yard, or the 'E1/Rs' at Barnstaple. And if there are memories of chill mist, bitter winds and driving rain, they are wiped out by even just one vision of blue sky, green bracken, riots of wild flowers, and the rich, lace-trimmed greens and blues of the Atlantic.

Let us leave it there, rather than list the stages down to the last day of the 'ACE' on 5 September 1964. If you want to dwell on the decline and collapse of it, there is some discussion in the next section, separated so that it will not spoil the portrait for those who prefer to look at the bright days.

Curtain

By 1963 the holiday train as a concept was being squeezed from three directions. The rich would, as always, choose the most comfort and convenience their money could buy, and if the motor car offered it they would choose it — always assuming that they would holiday in this country at all. There was the postwar boom in camping holidays, particularly among those who could not afford hotels, and camp sites were not going to be sited near railway stations. Then there were those who could just afford a nice car but then could not afford to pay train fares as well, so they had to use that car for all their travel, including holidays. These factors were a three-jawed vice around the 'ACE' and its ilk, and it was only a matter of time before it closed.

However, even without the tourist trade, the growth in population of Devon and Cornwall and the increasing demand for ease of movement might have promised ample business. It is customary, even now over 30 years after the event, to heap opprobrium on the British Railways Board and Dr Beeching, but there is no reason not to believe that had the people who lamented the scrapping of the West Country railways actually used them, they would still be with us.

Much has been made of politics and rivalries, but the basic reason for the disappearance of the 'ACE' and subsequently of the rest of the trains was simple: they were not wanted.

British Railways stated that it was not fair to regular passengers to make them support the facilities which were fully used only at holiday times. The holiday passengers were fast disappearing, doubtless sped by a helpful discourse from the President of the Town Planning Institute, Professor Colin Buchanan, who told an international meeting in Exeter on 2 September 1964 that Devon and Cornwall were no longer suitable venues for holidays. In any case, who other than that rare eccentric, the railway enthusiast, would enjoy being shunted backwards and forwards in a railway yard, when in a car he could be cruising swiftly through leafy lanes towards his destination?

Now that the country people all had cars, they believed that the railways no longer had any relevance to modern life, but were merely swallowing money they wanted for roads. In Wadebridge on 3 September, the MP for Truro said that it was better to spend money on improving roads for the benefit of all than on heavy subsidies for branch lines used by a few. Local lorry owners regarded the railway as an unfair competitor, supported by subsidies denied to them, and fought a long and costly campaign to drive it out. Transport Users' Consultative Committee meetings were held with the object of extracting promises from the Government that when the lines were closed the money saved would actually be applied to road improvements.

Reductions began with the commencement of the 1963 winter service, partly led by the rapid disappearance of the holiday passenger and partly driven by the policy of discarding the 2,000 or so coaches used only for a few trips in a year. The Bude, Torrington and Plymouth portions of the weekday train ceased to run. In summer 1964 they reappeared, but on Saturdays only. The two weekday and three Saturday trains between Waterloo and Exeter (there was no separate up Torrington train) continued to run until Saturday 5 September; Sunday had no 'ACE', and from Monday the 7th all Waterloo services terminated at Exeter St David's.

The plans presented in the summer of 1964 were for the closure of the branch lines, all the private sidings, most of the goods facilities and everything west of Okehampton. (The withdrawal of through services from Waterloo was not regarded as a closure, but was, like all changes associated with the Modernisation Plan, presented as an improvement.) The closures took over two years to effect, but eventually there were celebrations all over the West Country as last trains ran, the obstructions to field and road were pushed away and the station sites were turned into trading estates providing much-needed local jobs.

The passing of the 'ACE' elicited little more public interest than its arrival. Front-page news on 4 September 1964 was the opening of the Forth Road Bridge. On Monday the 7th the *Western Morning News*, which was anti-railway, printed a sentimental article, entitled 'Paddington takes over for "points West": Waterloo's last Atlantic', by railway writer & publisher David St John Thomas, who said that only enthusiasts would mourn its demise. The *Western Evening Herald* reported the closure, also from 7 September, of the St Budeaux (Victoria Road)–Devonport Junction section, also in sentimental vein. It also covered the last steam train on the Callington branch on the night of Saturday the 5th and the breakdown of the replacement diesel unit on the Monday morning. *The Times* was more sympathetic and on 16 November published a piece 'from a correspondent' under the title 'The Headlong Run to Salisbury'. It remarked on the lengthening of journey times which coincided with the new arrangement and the removal of steam power; then it briefly described a nonstop Waterloo–Salisbury run, and mentioned the 80min schedule but not the name.

Right: The 8.34am from Waterloo pulling out of Barnstaple Junction onto the Ilfracombe line on 1 July 1950; engine No 34034 *Honiton*. *A.F. Taylor*

Left: No 35022 *Holland-America Line* standing in the down middle road at Exeter Central after arrival. The livery of green with yellow stripes dates this view as 1949 or the first half of 1950. *Ian Allan Library*

Left: In the last summer, 1964, any old motive power would do. On 24 April the train is dividing at Exeter Central. 'N' class No 31846 has replaced the 'MN' No 35016 *Elders Fyffes*, which worked from London, and is ready to leave for Ilfracombe. The wooded bank behind the station is Northernhay Garden, originally the bailey of Rougemont Castle. *R.L. Sewell*

Below: A few minutes later No 34015 *Exmouth* has backed onto the Padstow portion. Beyond that, the restaurant set has been detached and drawn clear by a shunting engine. It is just possible to discern No 35016 retreating under Howell Road in the distance. *R.L. Sewell*

2

Operation

The Service

The number of stations served by this train, or rather collection of trains, varied from day to day and week to week. While it did, as an express, sweep through the smaller places from London to Salisbury, there was hardly a station on the entire Southern system west of Salisbury where an 'ACE' did not stop at some time or other. No wonder the operation was a trifle complex.

Between Waterloo and Exeter the one place where they always stopped was Salisbury. At first the down trains stopped nowhere else, but the up train called at Yeovil Junction and Surbiton. Woking and Basingstoke saw stops by one of the Saturday up trains. When the practice of connecting the Sidmouth and Exmouth coaches at Sidmouth Junction came in, that became a regular stop. At various times Andover Junction, Templecombe and Axminster also received one of the Saturday parts. When the name was restored after the war, the up train called at Sidmouth Junction, Axminster, Yeovil Junction, Sherborne and Templecombe. However, you could board the train at Waterloo and, by travelling in the coach detached at Salisbury and conveyed in the following stopping train, alight at all stations west thereof, with the sole exception of Sutton Bingham; whether these could be regarded as 'ACE' stations is a matter of opinion. Despite the insertion of these odd stops, the lesser places between Basingstoke and Exeter never had a satisfactory service. Moreover, putting variations into otherwise similar workings could be confusing, and was something of a tradition on this line. The writer has a treasured memory of a steam-hauled special, many years later, going slower and slower down into the Stour valley, while a lively discussion took place on the footplate over whether it should or should not stop at Gillingham.

Between Exeter and Barnstaple Junction the down train ran nonstop, whereas the up train stopped at all or most of the stations. Similarly, the down Plymouth train usually called at Okehampton, Tavistock and Devonport only, but Bere Alston, Lydford and Bridestowe often received the up train. Plymouth North Road was always in, as was Mutley before its demise. Even St Budeaux was in the final phase schedule, from 1962 onwards, up only; which shows that one should be careful about asserting that any station was not served by the 'ACE'. Yeoford and Crediton were sometimes in and sometimes out. The writer thinks that Tamerton Foliot and Ford were the only Devon stations where it never stopped, but would not care to be definite about this.

On the North Cornwall line the winter train called at all stations but the summer train usually called at only Launceston, Otterham, Delabole and Wadebridge. This was acceptable because another train, corresponding to the winter 'ACE', was then provided for the local travellers. On the Bude line, Dunsland Cross and Whitstone were omitted by the summer down train, but the up one included them.

There remain the branches: Lyme Regis, Seaton, Sidmouth, Exmouth; and Barnstaple to Ilfracombe. On these all the trains stopped at all the stations.

Incidentally, we may mention at this point the two branches which never had a through coach on the 'ACE' or any other London train: Callington, which in those days was not regarded as being on the tourist map, and Bodmin, the second town of Cornwall, whose treatment by the railways was disgraceful.

Making Up the Train

The formation of the train was determined by the timetable and by the order in which the portions divided or assembled. Each portion normally comprised a single Brake Composite coach (BCK), with the exception of Ilfracombe, the most important destination, which was nearly always served by a three-coach set. A restaurant set comprised a Kitchen/First Diner and a Third Diner, which always ran as a pair.

On the down train, it was a matter of uncoupling the rear coach or coaches in succession. Taking the winter 1937 formation as an example, the first division took place at

Salisbury, where the all-stations Exeter and the Seaton portions were taken off. This took place during the 5min stop when the train engine was changed. Then the 12.38pm Salisbury–Exeter, which had been waiting in the down sidings, backed into the platform and attached them. That train in turn left the Seaton coach at Seaton Junction, where the push-pull train which worked the branch ran through the main station to the up end, buffered onto the coach and propelled it down out of the platform, then drew into the branch platform for its 2.50pm departure.

The main train's next stop was at Sidmouth Junction to leave the Exmouth and Sidmouth coaches. Here the 2pm branch train stood in the loop called the 'middle siding' and, after the 'ACE' had moved off, it propelled onto the main line to attach the coaches. The branch train had its own division: at Tipton St John's the Exmouth coach was detached to wait for the 2.19pm Tipton–Exmouth train to back onto it.

On arrival at Exeter Central the train was divided into three. The restaurant set at the rear was uncoupled and, in due course, shunted into the down sidings to prepare for its return working. The train engine was removed and the first of two engines which had been waiting in the sidings overlooking the west incline backed onto the front portion and, only 6min after arrival, took it away to North Devon. The remainder departed for Plymouth behind the second engine 7min later.

In time the North Devon train reached Barnstaple Junction, to find the 'M7' and coach which formed the Torrington train, waiting on the short siding by the wall. The train pulled up short of the station, detached the Torrington coach and

Above: On 14 July 1964 a tired-looking No 31856 toils up to Central with part of the up 'ACE'. By the signal is a trap siding to arrest runaways on the incline. The sidings on the down side are packed with coaches, and another train is berthed on the up side. The timber merchants on the right are served by spurs off wagon turntables, an archaic survival at this time and one soon to disappear. *R.L. Sewel*

Right top to bottom: Three views showing the departure of the Plymouth portion from Okehampton. 2-6-0 No 31874 collects a coach from the yard, propels it towards the through portion in the platform, and moves out with the complete train. The engine was built at Woolwich in 1925 and is currently on the Mid-Hants Railway. The coach, No 1325, was built in 1933 and scrapped at the end of 1961. At the same time, a 'West Country' is shunting a train from the up platform to the bay for a Padstow service. This sequence was taken on Friday 7 July 1961. *Dr T. Gough*

31874

31874

31874

drew into Platform 2. In prewar years a Great Western coach was coupled onto the rear of the Ilfracombe portion to complete its journey. This coach had come down from Paddington on the 'Cornish Riviera Limited', been slipped from the latter at Taunton, brought to Barnstaple South Junction on the 1.10pm local, divided off and shunted round to the Junction, arriving at 3.18pm. The remarshalled train then departed, to turn sharp right over the River Taw and off up the formidable gradients of the Ilfracombe line. Meanwhile, the Torrington train backed through Platform 3 to pick up its coach.

The Plymouth train left the Padstow and Bude coaches at Okehampton. There, an engine which had just turned and refuelled at the little depot was in the yard on the down side, and worked those coaches forward to Padstow. At Halwill it detached the Bude coach, while the Bude branch train had to draw out of the station to the north until the main train had left, then propel in and collect the Bude coach.

Thus the formation at Waterloo was, from the concourse end: BCK Seaton, CK (Corridor Composite) Exeter, BCK Sidmouth, BCK Exmouth, Restaurant set, BCK Bude, BCK Padstow, BCK Plymouth, BCK Torrington, three-set Ilfracombe, engine. This normally made up to 13 coaches. After the war, when Padstow became the primary destination of the second section, the Plymouth coach was behind the Bude coach and was detached at Okehampton.

Joining the up portions together required shunt movements to extract the engine of the rear portion. The general routine was that the latter arrived first, its engine ran round it in the station and drew it back out of the way to allow the front portion to run in. It then propelled the through coach or coaches onto the back of the latter. At Halwill the Bude portion arrived first and shunted back onto the Bude line. At Okehampton the Plymouth portion did likewise and usually drew back into the military sidings, west of the station, to await the Padstow/Bude train, which followed it up from Meldon Junction. At Barnstaple Junction the Torrington portion arrived first and for the first few years drew back onto the branch, but later drew into the up siding, called the 'Shipyard' as it was the access to the Sawmilling & General Supplies Co yard on the waterside.

Exeter Central had a long platform with a central crossover to the through road. Here the Salisbury engine came down from Exmouth Junction depot, coupled up to the restaurant set and stood in the through road. The Cornwall train came in, ran up to the east end of the platform and its engine moved off. The North Devon train came up behind and its engine pulled out over the crossover. Then the Salisbury engine backed onto the Cornwall coaches, pushed them back to the North Devon coaches, and the whole train was united ready to go.

At Sidmouth Junction the train drew out of the platform until its tail end cleared the points, when the branch train propelled the Sidmouth and Exmouth coaches onto it. By this time the Seaton coach had been similarly attached at Seaton Junction to the 11.12am Exeter–Salisbury, which ran into Salisbury station at 2pm. When the 'ACE' arrived at 2.16 the shunting engine switched the coach from one to the other while they stood alongside.

What finally reached Waterloo was: engine, restaurant set, BCK Padstow, BCK Bude, BCK Plymouth, three-set Ilfracombe, BCK Torrington, BCK Exmouth, BCK Sidmouth, BCK Seaton — 12 coaches this time. For a postwar train, replace the last three by: Lyme Regis (attached Axminster) and Yeovil Town (attached Yeovil Junction).

It will be noted that under this scheme the diners had to make their way to the end of the train, and the noisy end at that. An alternative was to have a shunting engine at Exeter standing by on the west end of the restaurant set. After the arrival of the first portion, it pushed them over the central crossover onto the rear of it and then withdrew. The resultant formation was then: engine, BCK Padstow, BCK Bude, BCK Plymouth, restaurant set, three-set Ilfracombe, BCK Torrington, BCK Exmouth, BCK Sidmouth, BCK Seaton.

The above analyses refer to the true multi-portion train, which applied for most of the year. During the summer holidays the portions were expanded, by pairing each BCK with an Open Third (TO) or First/Third Composite (CK), adding two Corridor Thirds to each three-set to make it up to five, and so on, and then the formations east of Exeter were simpler. For instance, during August 1957, walking onto the platform at Waterloo you might see typically on one side the 11.0 — BCK Seaton, CK Exeter, restaurant set, TO & BCK Plymouth, TO and BCK Bude, three-set Padstow, engine; on the other side the 11.5 — BCK and CK Sidmouth, BCK Exmouth, TO and BCK Torrington, restaurant set, five-set Ilfracombe, engine.

In prewar years the heavy summer loads frequently required two engines from Exeter to the North Devon and North Cornwall routes. When there were assisting engines to be moved to or from Exmouth Junction depot, they were for preference attached to scheduled trains, so even a light train between Exeter and Yeoford or Okehampton could be seen with two engines. If there was also an extra engine for one of the westerly portions to be worked down from the depot, there would be three, and if on a busy day there was an Exeter Incline banking engine to be returned to St David's, a train would be seen pulling out of Exeter Central headed by four engines.

Above: The up Ilfracombe portion entering Barnstaple Junction on 24 August 1959. The Torrington line goes under the bridge to the left, and it is just possible to see the Torrington portion standing on the 'shipyard' siding beyond the bridge. *E.W.J. Crawforth*

Now, the above is simple enough, but it was usually necessary to have additional coaches to carry local passengers west of Exeter. These were generally found on the western, or down, end of the through coaches. On the down workings, the engines which took over portions at Exeter, Barnstaple Junction, Okehampton and Halwill would be waiting with the local coaches coupled to them. On the up working, at Barnstaple Junction the Torrington train pushed the through coach up to the main train, then drew back with the local coaches still coupled to the engine. From Bude, local coaches were run through to Okehampton, where they had to be dropped off before the Plymouth portion was coupled on. However, local coaches from Padstow or Ilfracombe to Exeter were placed at the fronts of their trains, so that the engine could pull them off after arrival at Central.

Thus you can have any number of combinations on the western 'ACEs'. Here are some examples:

Engine, two-set local Padstow, BCK Padstow, BCK Bude, two-set Plymouth (down Exeter–Okehampton);

Engine, five-set Ilfracombe, restaurant set Ilfracombe, three-set local, BCK Torrington (summer down, Exeter–Barnstaple);

Engine, restaurant set, three-set (summer Friday down, Halwill–Padstow);

Engine, two-set local Padstow, three-set Padstow, BCK Bude, two-set local Bude (up, Halwill–Okehampton);

Engine, two-set local Padstow, BCK Padstow, two-set local Bude, BCK Bude (down, Okehampton–Halwill);

Two engines, five-set, restaurant set, corridor third, two BCKs (summer Saturday down, Exeter–Camelford);

Engine, three-set Ilfracombe, BCK Torrington, bogie van Torrington (up, Barnstaple–Exeter with the empty newspaper van);

Engine, PMV van, two-set local, three-set Ilfracombe, GWR BCK (down, Barnstaple–Ilfracombe).

We could go on with these variations for quite a while, but probably the reader has got the general idea by now. Do not think that all train formations were like this; the marshalling of freight trains was much more complex.

All this coupling and uncoupling entailed a prodigious amount of work by the shunters. Even with Buckeye automatic couplers, it was necessary to unlatch the gangway connectors, duck underneath to uncouple the vacuum and heat hoses and lighting cable and stow them, then pull the coupler release chain while the train drew away. When joining up, the shunter had first to pull the coupler jaws open, lift a heavy collar off each buffer shank and push the buffer head in. Then once the vehicles were pushed together and movement had ceased, he had to check the coupler drop bolts, have the engine driver 'ease away' to check the coupler had locked, then couple up the cable and hoses. When coupling on an engine, he lifted the massive coupler to withdraw a pin, and swung it down out of the way; a normal drawhook thus revealed, he lifted over it the engine's screw coupling and tightened it up — and if you want a real arm-wrestling trial, try lifting an automatic coupler to the horizontal and holding it while pushing the pin back in. While doing all this, the shunter, walking about among moving trains, had to watch for his own safety. The driver, often some distance away, had to respond promptly to hand signals from the shunter, from the guard in carrying out a brake test, and from the fixed signals. The signalman, further off still in his box, had to handle his levers in correct sequence. If, for example, a coupler failed to engage, everyone had to know the procedure for substituting a screw coupling. The time allowed for joining up was usually 6min, sometimes less. That this was routine work carried out all over the railway, day or night, wet or dry, does not negate the fact that it was an immensely skilled operation.

All the passenger had to worry about was not ending up at the wrong destination. Great care was taken by the staff at Clapham Yard to put the correct roofboards on the coaches. A ticket inspector travelled from Salisbury to Exeter and checked where everyone was bound. Then before each coach was dropped off, the guard would walk through asking if everyone in it was for… , then lock the internal gangway doors.

To encourage passengers to be aboard in good time, the Southern made a practice of quoting the departure times from shorter stops at major stations as 2min earlier in the Public Timetable than in the Working Timetable. Thus, looking at winter 1947, Salisbury was shown as 12.33–12.38 Working and 12.33–12.36 Public, Exeter Central (Ilfracombe) was 2.29–2.36 Working and 2.29–2.34 Public, while Exeter Central (Plymouth), a longer stop, was 2.29–2.46 in both Working and Public. At minor stops, generally of half- or one-minute's duration, the arrival time was shown in the Public TT as the departure time; however, if the train was ready to leave at the Public departure time, the staff were permitted to send it off.

Below: The following sequence shows the down train dividing at Halwill Junction on Wednesday 5 July 1961. No 34011 *Tavistock*, working from Exeter to Padstow, pulls up in the platform.

Above right: It moves out with the two Waterloo–Padstow coaches and a Corridor Third put on at Exeter.

Centre right: The Bude train, 2-set No 168 and 'Standard' 2-6-2T No 82017, propels in to pick up its through coach.

Below right: This view of the departing Bude train shows the through coach to be Brake Composite No 6751. The North Cornwall line is the track disappearing to the left in front of the signal. *Dr T. Gough*

34011

168

Times and Speeds

Most accounts of train services discuss how they were speeded up over the years. A quest for more and more speed is now recognised as environmentally and socially damaging, and should have no place in a journey through the beauties of the West. On the other hand, people who live down there and wish to use the railway as their link with the rest of the country, might reasonably desire some advance over a decade or two, but that they did not see. That is not to say that efforts were not made to reduce journey times but on a route with steep gradients, sharp curves and frequent stops the overall speed is determined by the performance of the brakes and restrictions imposed by the track alignment, and those did not change.

The Working Time Table had a certain quaintness: for instance, the time between Tunnel Junction and Salisbury station was always shown, although it never changed from 2½min for all trains. In contrast, on a lot of nonstop trains there was only one intermediate time shown between Salisbury and Exeter, giving the impression that a crew could, if they wished, give it the works for half an hour and then stop to pick mushrooms. Farther west, the time between Barnstaple Town and Pottington never varied from 1min, but it was always quoted. One wonders why, for the amount of time you could gain or lose in 330yd could only be seconds, and no guard, however ferocious, was likely to book them.

The Exeter Central–St David's incline was always given 3min each way, as was St David's–Cowley Bridge. The 24-mile nonstop run thence to Okehampton, 34min in 1926, was 38min in 1962 with a stop at North Tawton. Okehampton–Meldon, 8min down (uphill) and 4min up, was typical of the shorter section timings which could hardly be reduced without a fantastic increase in installed power — and a line which ran 'West Country' class engines on three coaches can hardly be accused of underpowering its trains. However, there was surely room for improvement on the climb from Devonport to Okehampton; 58min before the war, it took 67min after, albeit with three more stops. It was not very fast for 32 miles. From Devonport King's Road station to Plymouth Friary the train reversed direction, taking 14min each way, although the stations were only 1⅝ miles apart across the city centre.

The 50 winding miles from Halwill to Padstow took 1hr 40min each way in 1926 and 1hr 27min in 1962, so some speed-up was attained as a result of a programme of permanent way improvement in the 1930s. However, remember that it was a single line, and where there are other trains to cross, a change in the schedule of one affects the others. The original up 'ACE', 8.35am from Padstow, had booked crossings at Tresmeer, Halwill and Ashbury, whereas in 1962 it was 8.30am with crossings at Wadebridge, St Kew Highway, Otterham and Halwill. The Saturday services, with more trains to be fitted together and loads two or three times as great, were generally slower on that account. The summer 1957 weekday down 'ACE' had only one crossing and took 1½hr, but the Saturday 10.35am and 11.15am down both had four, and took 1hr 53min.

The Bude branch was 18½ miles long and took 40min up and 34–38min down. Here again engine power had no effect on the permitted running speeds.

Exeter to Barnstaple, 40 miles, was run in 1hr 6min in 1926 and this varied by some 4min either way over the years. Barnstaple Junction and Town stations were separated by a 7-chain reverse curve, including the Taw Bridge, which took 3min to travel at 15mph. Then came the slog over Willingcott and, whether you were climbing the 1 in 40 from Braunton or the 1 in 36 from Ilfracombe, the following descent was taken very carefully: the running time for the 14 miles was, in the 1920s, 41min down and 37min up, and in the 1950s, 38min each way.

The Torrington line was another instance where the schedule was actually slowed during the life of the 'ACE', from 30 to 33min for the 14 mostly level miles.

The worst part was the ride in the Exmouth coach. It took an hour to go from Sidmouth Junction to Exmouth, 16½ miles by rail. The 1937 up timing was: 32min Exmouth–Tipton; 15min waiting there; 13min Tipton–Sidmouth Junction; 12min waiting there for the main train. No doubt this leisurely pace of travel is part of the charm of rural life and an ingredient of a good holiday.

What interested the passenger, whether Londoner anxious to escape from the city or country dweller wishing to get away to London, was the total journey time, and in this some improvement was offered over the first decade, only to be wiped out by the war and gradually retrieved again. There were innumerable variations; even in one year the Saturday trains all had different timings, generally resulting from the exigencies of finding paths for them at the London end. The following table shows some examples from the weekday 'ACEs':

Remember that these figures refer to the schedules laid down in the timetables. The actual effective running time was often less, as drivers made up time lost by temporary speed restrictions, unexpected traffic delays or over-running station stops. The allowance of 5–6min to water or change the engine, attach or detach vehicles, and load or unload quantities of baggage was often inadequate. It may also be worth reminding readers who drive cars that, although drivers were expected to regulate their speed within fairly precise limits, most locomotives were not equipped with speedometers.

There was another factor in the scheduling which may as well be mentioned here, as it was crucial in every sense of the word. Besides fitting together the crossings on the single lines and finding paths in the dense traffic east of Woking, there was Exeter. It is well known that the Southern trains passed through St David's station in the opposite direction to their Western counterparts, but the real significance of that is that at Exeter West and Cowley Bridge they had to cross the path of the Western traffic on flat junctions. This is a superb example of how the activities on one remote part of the railway system are profoundly related to those in other places many miles away. Not only was the timetable planned so that the two sets of services interlocked here, but in practice, trains which could be running well out of course had to be worked through this bottleneck. Small wonder that the Western signalmen regarded the task of their colleagues up at Central as 'child's play', while Southern staff were querulous over what was happening to their trains 'downstairs' on a busy day.

Waterloo to		**Ilfracombe**	**Plymouth**	**Padstow**
		hr-min	*hr-min*	*hr-min*
Summer 1926	down	5-24	5-16	6-31
	up	5-22	5-18	7-4
Winter 1926–7	down	5-29	5-27	6-59
	up	5-38	5-34	7-25
Summer 1937	down	5-0	5-3	5-49
	up	5-10	5-36	6-32
Winter 1937–8	down	5-6	5-10	6-37
	up	5-19	5-28	7-9
1940	down	5-40	5-56	7-29
	up	6-10	5-56	–
Summer 1952	down	5-10	5-15	5-54
	up	5-10	5-38	6-33
Summer 1962	down	5-55	5-22	6-0
	up	4-59	5-19	5-48

Left: Seaton Junction. Having collected the Seaton coach, the driver of the branch train brings it into the platform while the signalman is about to hand the single-line tablet to his mate. At this time, 8 August 1960, the Seaton train comprised 'M7' No 30048 and coaches Nos 6675 and 1320. *Dr T. Gough*

On a summer Saturday in 1937, the 10.30am Paignton–Liverpool and the 7.30am Paddington–Kingswear passed each other at Cowley Bridge at 11.53, just 2min before the first up 'ACE' crossed over. The latter stopped in the station at 11.58 and pulled out at 12.2, turning left up the hill, then the Kingswear train went at 12.4. Meanwhile the 10.20am Paignton–Birmingham headed north at 12.0. The 7.45am Penzance–Wolverhampton arrived at 12.5 and left at 12.14, at which time the second up 'ACE' was running in to Cowley Bridge to cross in front of it, slotting in 2min behind the 8.10am Birmingham–Paignton. There followed on the down line the 9am Paddington–Paignton and the 9.30am Paddington–Perranporth, then the 11.50am Torquay–Paddington passed through nonstop, and as soon as it was clear, the third up 'ACE' came in. Even as that was pulling into the station, an auto-train was setting off up to Dulverton and the 5.30am Pontypool–Newton freight train was due over the junction.

At 1.50pm the first of the five down 'ACEs' came down the incline and the others followed at 2.3, 2.11, 2.23 and 2.31, interspersed with the 12.5pm Kingswear-Manchester at 2.4, 1pm Paignton–Wolverhampton at 2.14, 10.15am Penzance–Crewe at 2.20, and 2.10pm Dawlish-Exeter at 2.31. The last was booked to run into the up relief as the 'ACE' was entering the up middle. At least in this direction down Southern trains did not conflict with down GW trains at Cowley Bridge.

And so it went on throughout the day. It would be demanding far too much of human nature to expect that everything would run precisely to time. Even if it did, with these nominal 2min spacings it was inevitable that many trains would be checked here, sufficient to give credence to enthusiasts' tales that GW men deliberately stopped Southern trains to assert their ownership. The little signalbox perched above the river, opposite the garden of the Cowley Bridge Inn, was indeed the focal point of West Country transport, and that it worked so well was an achievement as wondrous as any in the region's history.

The Dash To Exeter

Wheels may turn to a measured pace in far Cornwall, but the 'ACE' was a quite different kind of train east of Exeter Central — a full-blown express. Waterloo to Salisbury is 83 miles 56 chains, Salisbury to Sidmouth Junction is 75 miles 73 chains, and Salisbury to Exeter is 88 miles 4 chains. These were the sections over which the enthusiasts enthused about how fast the engine driver could go.

However, the railway companies were as capable as anyone else of pulling the statistical wool over the public's eyes, and the fact that of the multitude of 'ACEs', the up trains were usually slower than the down and the Saturdays slower than the weekdays, was obscured. For example, in the halcyon summer of 1937, the Saturday up Ilfracombe/Torrington ran up from Salisbury in 87min, while the first Padstow/Bude took 94min, the second Padstow took 92min, and the Plymouth/Bude followed in a sedate 109min — hardly a breakneck pace even with an 'S15' class engine! In the last decade the Saturday up timings from Exeter to Salisbury were: Ilfracombe 107min, Torrington 110min, Bude 101min, Padstow 95min. Even in 1962 the Saturday down trains were allowed between 104-110min from Exeter to Salisbury, whereas before the war they were all at 98min.

The star turns were the 11am down from Waterloo and the 12.30pm up from Exeter (or equivalents). The opposite table is a selection of times.

Above: The view southwards from Tipton St John's shows the Sidmouth line rising to the left and the Exmouth line curving away level to the right. Standard 2-6-2T is bringing in the 10.20am from Sidmouth while the 9.52am from Exmouth waits in the background, on 3 August 1959. These two trains had through coaches to Waterloo, not by the 'ACE' but by the 10.30am from Exeter. *S.C. Nash/E.W.J. Crawforth Collection*

	Wloo–Sals		Sals–Exe		Sals–Sid Jn		Exe–Sals		Sid Jn–Sals		Sals–Wloo	
	min	*mph*	*min*	*mph*	*min*	*mph*	*min*	*mph*	*min*	*mph*	*min*	*mph*
1926	90	55.8	100	52.9	-	–	102	51.9	–	-	90	55.8
1937	86	58.4	96	55.0	83	54.9	98	53.9	85	53.6	86	58.4
1940	103	48.8	110	48.0	91	50.0	128	41.3	103	44.2	101	49.8
1947	103	48.8	111	47.6	90	50.6	138	38.3	114	40.0	95	52.9
1957	83	60.4	97	54.5	79	57.6	99	53.5	79	57.6	85	59.1
1962	80	62.8	93	56.9	75	60.6	93	56.9	74	61.5	80	62.8

Sidmouth Junction to Exeter, just over 12 miles, was run in 13min pass to stop in 1926 and 14min start to stop in later years, which, since it included the descent through Black Boy Road Tunnel into Central station, was quite exhilarating, and at the bridge over the River Clyst trains were going very fast indeed; as a feat of haulage it was not so wonderful as most of it was downhill at 1 in 100 and 1 in 145. The up run over that section was generally allowed 18min, which was pretty hard going when starting cold out of Exeter, and meant that you had to have the fire correct from the beginning.

In the difficult period after the war the schedules were actually slower than they had been during it, on account of the backlog of maintenance on the track. At that time the new 'Merchant Navy' and 'West Country' class engines were coming into use in numbers, and these just toyed with most of the jobs given to them; a driver who opened one out, either to liven up the fire or just for fun, soon found himself embarrassingly ahead of time. At that time the well-known driver Fred Prickett, who did not approve of running early, had an argument on his footplate with a design office representative, who wanted him to use full regulator. Eventually he did so, while travelling at 70mph, but he had to ease off within a matter of seconds as she leapt up to 90. Clearly the management, and the passengers, expected something quicker.

The 83min timing for the eastern half was instigated in 1952 during a general speed-up. For the next 10 years the 11am down 'ACE', which ran to this timing, was the only train on the entire Southern Region booked to run at over a mile-a-minute average from start to stop. What is so special about that figure? Nothing; but it impresses the public and, more importantly, the politicians who know nothing about railways but hold the purse-strings. And as the years went by, the other regions posted more and more trains over this magic 60 figure, and then over 70 as well, while the Southern still had just the one.

It is in this context that we come to the final fling: the 23 August 1961 acceleration which gave 62.8mph Waterloo–Salisbury, 60.6mph Salisbury–Sidmouth Junction, 61.5mph Sidmouth Junction–Salisbury and 62.8mph Salisbury–Waterloo. The first down train to the new timings carried a goodly complement of enthusiasts, and the 'Merchant Navy' *Clan Line* delighted them by arriving at Exeter 2min early,

Below: Concluding another 'ACE' run to Exeter, a junior Exmouth Junction driver takes No 35014 *Nederland Line* back from Central station to the shed for turn-round servicing on 4 May 1964. *A. Swain*

Left: Preparing an engine for the road, a junior fireman is on the tender tidying up the heap of coal which has been dropped from the overhead coaling plant. His surroundings — non-existent roof, broken windows — are typical of postwar conditions at the sheds. The photograph is dated 20 September 1948. *British Railways/MNLPS Collection*

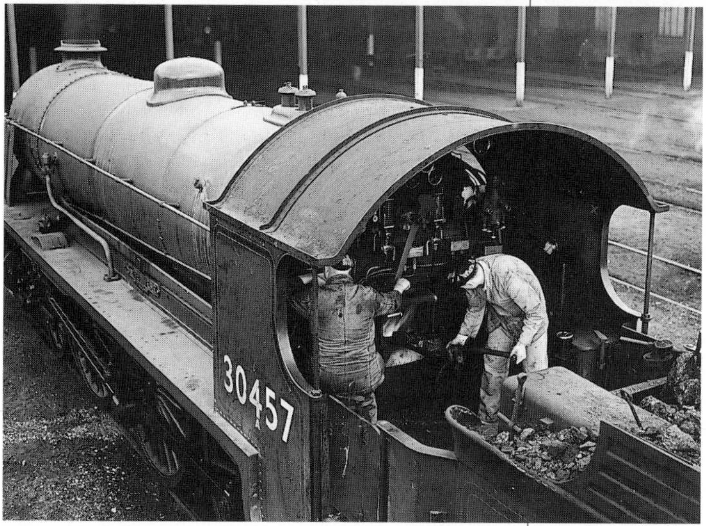

Below left: A photograph, dated 2 October 1952, of an engine crew in action, but of course they are stationary in Nine Elms engine shed. Their engine, No 30457 *Sir Bedivere* is a second series 'N15', built at Eastleigh in 1925. It is a pity no one thought to clean off the streaks of scum below the boiler washout plug, and one hopes the plug is not leaking but has just been put in after a washout. *British Railways/MNLPS Collection*

Right: After the posed shots, this is the real thing: total concentration. Driver Prickett on 'MN' No 35019 *French Line CGT* at speed. *MNLPS Collection*

having run the 172 miles in 165min. One month later, Driver Burridge of Exmouth Junction let the same engine go down from Hewish to Axminster and reached 104mph; this was the highest speed ever recorded by stop-watch timing on the West of England line.

Since there was no real reduction in journey times to the resorts, this rescheduling was pure window dressing, but it was good publicity. Moreover, it enabled the Southern to boast of getting to Exeter in less than 3hr — 2hr 58min. There was even talk of beating the fastest steam-hauled timing which the Western Region had achieved, of 2hr 52min, but the proposed 2hr 48min schedule was never implemented. This glorious Indian summer lasted for three years, for in the meantime the British Railways Board decided it should not provide two lots of express services between London and Exeter, and 5 September 1964 saw the end, not only of the 'ACE', but of all fast nonstop running on the route.

Of course, the concept of a railway as a race track belongs to a certain breed of passenger and not to railwaymen, whose aim is to get through their working day without being accused of causing unpunctuality. Having said that, the small band of men who drove and fired these crack trains were, in the main, keen to get the best from their engines; such men could be scathing when they found themselves on a Saturday morning being held up by the Feltham crew on the 10.35 who, concerned about getting steam or lacking the confidence to let her rip down towards Salisbury Spire before putting the brake on for Tunnel Junction, lost time. This run was a very demanding one. With a speed limit of 60mph out to Malden, the eastern half of the down run then demanded an hour's hard steaming at 70–80mph with no let-up. The up run was not so bad, provided one was blessed

with a good start out of Salisbury, for the fireman would not normally expect to put any more coal on after Woking. On the switchback western half the driver had to be willing to run well up to the 85mph limit through the dips, and if he still was not on time he would have to thrash the engine up the inclines. Many a fireman has sweated to get a fire back in the box, the water back up the glass and the steam back round the clock, before seeing his driver put the lot out of the chimney on the next upgrade.

Moreover, driving a fast steam train on a line like this was a task so demanding as to be approaching the limit of human aptitude. In the 48min run from Waterloo to Basingstoke the driver had to see, identify, read and obey 113 running signals — one every 26sec on average. In bad conditions of heavy rain, dust or haze he might have but 5-6sec in sight of each one, and could also be faced with exhaust steam from his engine blowing into his already limited field of view. Indeed, at the automatic signals between Woking and Basingstoke, which were aligned centrally above the track, drivers were accustomed to having to shut off steam in order to read them. This in addition to judging his speed, keeping an eye on how well his mate was supplying him with steam, remembering any special instructions such as temporary speed limits, knowing exactly where he was and when to start reducing speed for stops, and so on. He could receive little help from the fireman, for as we have remarked the latter was pretty busy with the shovel. It took an exceptional man to tackle this job, and to those concerned with the problem of driving workload, the arrival of diesel and electric locomotives came as an answer to prayer.

Travelling further west, the difficulty in scheduling fast trains became, in some sense, the converse: the distance between signalboxes. The Absolute Block Signalling Regulations prohibit a signalman from allowing a train to pass his home signal until he has been advised that the previous train has passed the next signalbox ahead. Because the Government regulations require mechanically-worked points to be within 350yd of the box, the boxes are perforce sited at stations, unless the railway is prepared to go to the expense of building and manning extra boxes purely to shorten the sections. The only one of that kind between Salisbury and Exeter was midway up Honiton Incline. The two most widely spaced boxes on the route in 'ACE' days were Gillingham and Templecombe, 6 miles 64 chains apart. Thus with two trains averaging 60mph 7min apart, the first should pass Templecombe just as the second was approaching Gillingham. In practice, you must allow time for the Templecombe signalman to send the telegraph message to his colleague and for the latter to pull off his signals. If the second train came within sight of the Gillingham distant signal before it had been pulled off, its driver would put his brake on and come slowly up to the home, ready to stop. He would thus take much longer to go through the section, and if another train was running close behind him, it could well be stopped altogether at Semley, the next box to the east, resulting in a cumulative hold-up along the line. Therefore 9min was the minimum practical headway on this part of the line, and in the schedules we see, for instance, the 10.35 and 10.38 departures from Waterloo spaced out to pass Yeovil Junction at 12.49 and 12.58. Even at that it was important that the second driver did not overhaul the train in front, for, apart from any other consideration, stopping and starting consumes more fuel, and that costs the railway money!

Locomotive Duties

The headquarters of locomotive operation for the West of England was the main depot at Exmouth Junction. It employed over 400 men and was a big industrial unit by any standards. The depots at Plymouth Friary, Wadebridge and Barnstaple generally covered only their local areas. Smaller still were the sheds at Lyme Regis, Seaton, Exmouth, Ilfracombe, Okehampton and Bude, with only two or three engine crews and a couple of shed men based on

each. In the summer more men were allocated to the outlying depots, and to accommodate the crews of the numerous summer extra trains, some ex-LNWR coaches were placed at Padstow, Bude, Seaton and Lyme Regis, the last named having a sumptuous 12-wheeler in later years. London–Exeter expresses were shared roughly equally with Nine Elms depot. Salisbury depot's men took part in working the 'ACE'; before the war its engines worked the Salisbury–Exeter leg, but when through working was introduced they were no longer involved.

The major change in the pattern of working over the years was an increase in the mileage obtained from individual engines. Before the war the engines working from Exeter to Ilfracombe, Plymouth and Padstow generally stabled overnight (at Wadebridge in the last case) and did the up working next morning. When the majority of the engines available were of the 4-4-0 type, two were needed on the heavier loads between Barnstaple and Ilfracombe, from Okehampton to Camelford or from Wadebridge to Okehampton, and these additional engines were of course surplus for much of the time. However, in those days it was normal to store them, and even to lay off staff, during the winter months. Later on, the 'ACE' was taken in the course of more complex and varied duties, and the same engine seldom appeared on the same train on consecutive days. The Southern regarded all its engines as 'mixed-traffic' capable, and many duties included both passenger and freight haulage. Similarly, the footplate crews in Devon and Cornwall covered all kinds of work, including preparation and disposal, shunting, local or express trains, in the course of a turn.

Above: The up 'ACE' ascending the 1 in 36 incline from Ilfracombe in the beautiful Slade valley. The first coach is a BR Standard, the second a Bulleid, and among the differences will be noted the positioning of the destination boards. The engine is No 34066 *Spitfire*. *Ian Allan Library*

From 1926 to 1952 engines were usually changed at Salisbury. The London engine and crew, on Nine Elms Duty No 7, worked the 'ACE' down and back. Salisbury to Exeter was part of Salisbury Duty No 472, which covered the down newspapers, 6.30am Exeter–Salisbury, down 'ACE' and 4.30pm back; the up working was similar. Regular through engine working between Waterloo and Exeter was tried in 1933, but then it also involved the crew working through and lodging away overnight, which was not popular and probably caused its cessation.

In the postwar era the Waterloo–Exeter engine on the 11am returned on an evening van train to Clapham Junction. The 12.30pm Exeter–Waterloo engine returned on the 10.15pm freight from Nine Elms to Exeter. When the 11.5am down and 12.18pm up ran in summer, they were worked alternately by Nine Elms and Exmouth Junction engines, which went up one day and down the next. On all these, the London half was worked by Nine Elms or Salisbury men and the Exeter half by Exmouth Junction men. During the crew change at Salisbury the engine was watered and the coal in the tender pushed forward, this being allowed the same 5-6min as the previous engine change.

The Salisbury-Exeter stopper was worked as far as Yeovil Junction by Salisbury men on a Nine Elms 'West Country' on Duty 23, which came down on the 7.20am Waterloo–Salisbury and returned to London on a milk train. It was taken forward to Exeter by another 'West Country', which was on a complex three-day diagram including overnight stops at Barnstaple and Salisbury. The 11.12 Exeter–Salisbury had a 'West Country' working through from Ilfracombe to Yeovil Junction, with Yeovil men, then a Yeovil-based 2-6-0 on Duty 512, which would subsequently shunt Salisbury East Yard in the afternoon, do a trip to Milford, take the 4.25pm from Cardiff forward to Portsmouth and via three other trains, get back to Yeovil shed at 4.40 the following morning. This engine was taken to Templecombe by Yeovil men, who changed there with a Salisbury crew.

The Exeter–Padstow portion was hauled by a 'West Country', Exmouth Junction Duty 581, which had come up on the 8.25am from Plymouth and went on Wadebridge depot overnight. This same engine took up Duty 582 the following morning. It started work on the 7.20am Wadebridge–Padstow goods train, worked the 8.30am up 'ACE' to Exeter, then took the Exeter–Ilfracombe portion down, and finished by working home to Exmouth Jn on the 5.25pm Torrington–London freight.

In summer, when the 8.30am was merely an all-stations train to Exeter, the up Padstow 'ACE' left at around 9.35. The engine for that was also stabled at Wadebridge and came down coupled to the 7.53am passenger train. It was taken as far as Camelford by Wadebridge men, who there changed mounts with the Okehampton men arriving with the 8.15am Launceston– Wadebridge goods train. The latter took it to Okehampton, where they went off to take over the 'T9' which shunted there for most of the day. From Okehampton to Exeter it was in the charge of an Exmouth Junction crew, who had worked down on the 6.55am freight. This arrangement, the most complex involving the 'ACE', was typical of the elaborate interlocking movements of engines and men that went on all over the railway. Incidentally, although it has nothing to do with the 'ACE', the next train out of Padstow, the 12.58pm, went only as far as Wadebridge before the engine was changed. This cannot have given the passenger much of an impression of the reliability of the South Western 'Greyhounds'.

The engine which worked the up train from Ilfracombe was on Duty 556; off Exmouth Junction shed at 4.35am to pick up the paper train at 5.6am at Central. Arriving at Ilfracombe at 6.50, it spent the next 2½hr marshalling the coaches, then was turned and refuelled for the 10.30 departure. On arriving at Exeter again at 12.24pm, the crew, who had been on duty since 4.20am, were relieved at the station. The engine hauled the 1.10pm stopping train to Yeovil Junction, turned there, took the 3.20pm Exeter to Templecombe and worked the 6pm freight back to Exeter.

The down Torrington portion was picked up at Barnstaple Junction by a Barnstaple 'M7', which returned double-heading on the 4.37pm from Torrington. It had spent the morning working the 6.30am Barnstaple-Torrington freight, including shunting out Bideford goods depot and, while at Torrington, moving the up 'ACE' stock into the platform. The latter was taken out by an engine, an 'M7' or latterly one of the LMSR-type 2-6-2Ts, which was on a long day: starting at 4.45am with a Barnstaple-Torrington freight, the 2.6am from Exeter; the 6.25 mixed train down to Petrockstowe on the North Devon and Cornwall Junction and back to Torrington; then four Torrington-Barnstaple round trips, and back to shed at 10pm.

The Bude branch was largely covered from Okehampton; an 'N' class 2-6-0 on Duty 594 went down on the 4.37am freight, did the 7.58am passenger to Halwill and 8.53am back, turned on the Bude turntable and got the 'ACE' coaches out of the siding. Having delivered them to Halwill it returned to Holsworthy with a brake van to work the 12.10pm freight to Exeter. The down 'ACE' was taken on by a tank engine, for years an 'M7', from 1952 a BR Standard 2-6-2T, which was based on Bude's little shed and did five round trips to Halwill.

The Plymouth duty was another engine on a mixed turn, lasting two days. It left Friary shed at 8.10am to work the 8.20 freight to Exeter and the 9.20pm freight from there to Yeoford. It shunted at Yeoford all night, leaving with the 3.35am freight to Tavistock and the 6am passenger from there to Plymouth. After engine requirements on Friary shed, it was brought up by Plymouth men on the 11.5am freight to Okehampton, turned at Okehampton and took the Plymouth 'ACE' portion down with an Okehampton crew. The engine for the up Plymouth portion left Exmouth Junction in the early morning and ran light to Okehampton, thence to work the 7am passenger train to Plymouth. On returning to Okehampton with the 'ACE', it spent the afternoon on a round trip to Bude and then stayed on Okehampton shed overnight. The up 'ACE' was taken by Plymouth men; the engine was usually a 4-4-0 or an 'N' class, although 'West Countries' were sometimes used.

The Sidmouth and Exmouth branches were worked by engines and men from Exmouth Junction, spending their shifts in fairly complex procedures covering the branches, Exeter–Honiton locals and shunting at Exeter Central. The engine which worked the through coach down to Sidmouth worked the branch goods back to Exmouth Junction. Seaton and Lyme Regis had little engine sheds where engines were stabled overnight, and each had two sets of men based on them. On these two lines the weekday passenger timetable could be covered by one engine with two crews. Working on the country branches was not a bucolic idyll. The Seaton early turn lasted 8hr 20min and included nine return trips, and the late turn comprised seven or eight round trips and disposal. A real fun day must have been the late turn on Yeovil Duty 517: sign on at 2.20pm to traverse the 2-mile Junction–Town branch 24 times until getting relief soon after 10pm.

As the summer Saturday service built up, it was necessary to find extra engines, and here the Southern was fortunate in that the types it used for freight traffic, such as the 'K10' 4-4-0s, 'N' 2-6-0s, 'S15' 4-6-0s and Bulleid Pacifics, were suitable for transferring to passenger duties. For example, in the final phase — the late 1950s and early 1960s — the 10.48am from Torrington was taken forward from Barnstaple Junction by a Barnstaple-based 'West Country', which during the week was on local freight work. This engine returned with the down Ilfracombe train. Exmouth Junction had to find another 'West Country' for a Saturday-only duty which included the 10.30am up from Ilfracombe.

Waterloo-Exeter duties encompassing the 'ACEs' were as follows: No 6 — 11am down, 5.45pm up; No 9 — 12.15am down, 1.45pm up; No 16 — 7.30am down, 2.12pm up; No 19 — 11.15am down, 6.48pm up; No 529 — 12.45pm up; No 530 — 12.30pm up.

On some summer Saturdays the down Padstow/Bude train changed engines at Salisbury; it was worked from and to Waterloo by a Nine Elms engine with a Feltham crew, from Exeter to Salisbury by an Exmouth Junction engine on Duty No 554, and from Salisbury to Exeter by a Salisbury engine on Duty No 492. The latter was the only postwar appearance of a Salisbury engine on an 'ACE'.

Another feature of summer Saturdays was that the heavier loads would need banking assistance. The up train was banked out of Ilfracombe by an 'N' class, which was a Barnstaple duty; for the down train the banker was a 'West Country', which had come down from Exmouth Junction to work the extra 8.10am up to Exeter and 1.12pm back. The Exeter St David's–Central bank saw a variety of engines, including 'M7s', the 'E1/R' class (which was a 'Brighton' 0-6-0T fitted with a larger coal bunker and extra rear wheels to increase its range) and in the last five years the 'Z' class 0-8-0Ts and 'W' class 2-6-4Ts. In view of the sharp curve on the exit from St David's station, there was an instruction that the banker must push gently until clear of the pointwork.

For moving empty trains between Waterloo and Clapham Yard a squad of tank engines was employed; for many years 'T1', 'M7' or 'O2' classes. In 1959 some Great Western pannier tanks were brought in to make up a shortfall until BR Standard tanks became available. From 1932 until 1950 the important task of shunting coaches in Clapham Yard was performed by the unique 0-8-0T No 949 *Hecate*. This engine was built by Hawthorn Leslie for the Kent & East Sussex Railway and acquired by the Southern in exchange for one more suited to that line. Elsewhere, the duties were arranged so that all the shunting, freight as well as passenger, was performed by train engines in between their other workings. The exceptions were Barnstaple Junction and Devonport King's Road, where an engine was available all day for shunting, and Wadebridge. Here one of the three celebrated Class 0298 Beattie well tanks shunted around the station all day, while another went off to collect the clay wagons from Wenford Bridge and the third rested in the shed.

Generally unobserved by the travelling public, but of paramount importance, was the vast amount of work that went on at the engine sheds — the preparation and disposal of engines ('P&D'). This work (which was discussed in detail in the author's *From the Footplate: Atlantic Coast Express*) comprised basically examination and oiling, raising steam and building up the fire, then at the end of the run cleaning or dropping the fire, removing ash and taking coal and water. At Nine Elms, Exmouth Junction and Barnstaple there were P&D duties allocated to junior

enginemen; elsewhere the work was carried out by crews as a part of their daily round, and the engine they prepared might be the one on which they worked the rest of the turn or it might not. It was important to make a good job of preparing an engine to be taken out by another crew; you would also be working engines which someone else had prepared for you.

Top & above: On Saturday 23 July 1962, an unspecified up train moves out of Exeter St David's onto the incline to Central, hauled by No 34056 *Croydon* and pushed with due caution by 'Z' class No 30956. The wall on the left with the notice is the original South Devon Railway carriage shed, hence the designation of 'South Devon Sidings' on the notice. *Ian Allan Library*

Above: This sort of power was not needed on any train, so No 34034 *Honiton* was probably being tripped westwards for another job on 16 June 1959, and for convenience was coupled to the train being hauled by No 34032 *Camelford.* The pair are pulling out of Exeter St David's over Red Cow Crossing; on the left is the crossing keeper's hut below Exeter Middle signalbox. *A.M. Lawrence*

Left: One seldom opened a Bulleid Pacific full out, but here is No 34060 *25 Squadron* being given the lot up Ilfracombe incline, approaching Campscott cutting. *R. Russell*

Right top: The lovely country setting of Seaton Junction. At 2.30pm on 4 September 1952, the 1.25pm Exmouth Junction–Salisbury freight comes down the bank. The engine is 'S15' No 30843. On the left the stock of a Seaton excursion is berthed in the siding. *J. Hollington*

Below: Journey's end at Padstow. On 1 July 1961 No 34033 *Chard* has hooked off and is moving forward to the stops to run round. This is a Saturday and the two-coach set has been augmented by a loose Corridor Third. The bus outside bound for Newquay is a descendant of the South Western's ambition to get its trains there. *Dr T. Gough*

Bottom: On the same day, No 31837 with empty coaches in front of the fish shed. This siding extended round to the harbour, but was mostly used for berthing coaches. *Dr T. Gough*

Examples of 'ACE' Times

	Summer 1926 Down			Up			Winter 1926	
	M-S	*M-F*	*SO*	*M-S*	*M-F*	*SO*	*M-S*	*M-S*
Waterloo	d 11.0	d 11.10	d 10.25	a 3.44	a 3.39	a 4.29	d 11.0	a 4.0
Ilfracombe	a 4.24			d 10.22			a 4.29	d10.22
Bude		a 4.42	a 3.37		d 9.45	d 11.0	a 4.57	d 9.45
Padstow		a 5.41	a 4.35		d 8.35	d 10.0	a 5.59	d 8.35
Plymouth	a 4.29			d 10.15			a 4.40	d 10.15
Exmouth		a 4.0		d 10.40				d 11.40
Sidmouth		a 3.24			d 11.15			d 12.10

Summer 1937 — Down

	M-F	*M-F*	*SO*	*Q SO*	*SO*	*SO*	*Q SO*	*SuO*
Waterloo	d 10.35	d 11.0	d 10.35	d 10.38	d 10.41	d 11.0	d 11.6	d 10.45
Ilfracombe	a 3.35		a 3.34	a 3.52				a 3.54
Torrington	a 3.30					a 4.15	a 4.15	a. 3.45
Bude	a 3.26	a 4.54				a 4.12		
Padstow	a 4.24	a.5.36			a 4.53			
Plymouth		a 4.13				a 4.22		
Seaton		a 3.2						
Lyme Regis		a 3.6						

Summer 1937 — Up

	M-F	*M-F*	*SO*	*SO*	*SO*	*SO*	*SuO*	*SuO*
Waterloo	a 3.40	a 4.12	a 3.34	a 3.41	a 4.33	a 4.42	a 3.50	a 3.58
Ilfracombe	d 10.30		d 10.10	d10.30			d 10.30	d 10.30
Torrington	d10.28		d 10.22				d 10.28	d 10.28
Bude	d 9.40	d 10.40	d 9.40		d 10.40			
Padstow	d 8.40	d 9.40	d 8.40			d 10.25		
Plymouth		d 10.25			d 10.35			d 10.20
Exmouth		d 12.1						d11.48
Sidmouth		d 12.35						d 12.18

Winter 1937

	Down	*Up*
	M-S	*M-S*
Waterloo	d 11.0	a 3.34
Ilfracombe	a 4.6	d 10.30
Torrington	a 3.58	d 10.28
Bude	a 4.39	d 9.40
Padstow	a 5.37	d 8.40
Plymouth	a 4.20	d 10.10
Exmouth	a 2.46	d 11.50
Sidmouth	a 2.23	d 12.20
Seaton	a 3.2	d 11.50

	1 Jan 1940				1942 Code P.X.		1942 Code P.Y.	
	Down	*Up*	*Down*	*Up*	*Down*	*Up*	*Down*	*Up*
	M-S	*M-S*	*SuO*	*SuO*				
Waterloo	d 10.50	a 2.25	d 11.0	a 4.10	d 11.0	a 4.10	d 11.0	a 5.30
Ilfracombe	a 4.30	d 8.15			a 5.26	d 9.50	a 6.48	d 10.25
Bideford						d 10.2		
Torrington	a 4.31	d 8.15			a 5.20		a 6.31	d 10.22
Bude	a 5.9	d 8.2			a 5.23	d 9.48	a 6.50	d 9.40
Launceston		d 8.22						
Padstow	a 6.19				a 6.39	d 8.30	a 7.54	d 8.30
Plymouth	a 4.57	d 8.20	a 5.12	d 10.0	a 5.12	d 10.0	a 6.36	d 10.10

	Summer 1947						Winter 1947	
	Down			*Up*				
	M-S	*SO*	*SO*	*M-F*	*SO*			
Waterloo	d 10.50	d 10.20	d 10.35	a 4.41	a 3.55	a 4.41	d 10.50	a 4.41
Ilfracombe	a 4.36		a 4.10	d 10.15		d 10.15	a 4.36	d 10.15
Torrington	a 4.31		a 4.0	d 10.15		d 10.5	a 4.31	d 10.15
Bude	a 5.9	a 3.55		d 9.35	d 9.35		a 5.9	d 9.35
Padstow	a 6.21	a 5.0		d 8.25	d 8.25		a 6.21	d 8.25
Plymouth	a 4.55						a 4.55	
Exmouth	a 3.17						a 3.17	
Sidmouth	a 2.48						a 2.48	
Seaton	a 3.27						a 3.27	

Summer 1952 — Down

	M-F	*Q M-F*	*SO*	*SO*	*SO*
Waterloo	d 11.0	d 11.5	d 10.22	d 10.54	d 11.0
Ilfracombe	a 4.10			a 4.36	
Torrington	a 4.4			a 4.30	
Bude	a 3.52		a 3.54		a 5.9
Padstow	a 4.54		a 5.0		a 6.22
Plymouth	a 4.30	a 4.30			a 4.56
Exmouth	a 2.51	a 2.51			
Sidmouth	a 2.27	a 2.27			
Seaton	a 3.27	a 3.27			

Summer 1952 — Up

	M-F	*M-F*	*SO*	*SO*	*SO*	*Q SO*	*SO*
Waterloo	a 3.40	a 4.13	a 3.23	a 3.53	a 4.19	a 5.37	a 5.42
Ilfracombe	d 10.30			d 10.30	d 10.48		
Torrington	d 10.30						
Bude	d 9.30	d 10.40	d 9.30			d 11.45	d 11.45
Padstow	d 8.30	d 9.40	d 8.30				d 10.45
Plymouth	d 9.50						
Lyme Regis	d 11.40						
Yeovil	d 12.42						

	Winter 1961		Summer 1962 — Down				
	Down	*Up*					
	M-S	*M-S*	*M-F*	*Q M-F*	*SO*	*SO*	*SO*
Waterloo	d 11.0	a 3.29	d 11.0	d 11.5	d 10.35	d11.0	d 11.15
Ilfracombe	a 3.55	d 10.30	a 3.55			a 4.38	
Torrington	a 3.49	d 10.30	a 3.49			a 4.31	
Bude	a 4.16	d 9.30	a 4.12	a 4.12	a 3.54		a 5.7
Padstow	a 5.21	d 8.30	a 5.0	a 5.0	a 5.0		a 6.22
Plymouth	a 4.22	d 10.2	a 4.22	a 4.22			a 4.47
Exmouth	a 2.27		a 2.27				
Sidmouth	a 2.6		a 2.6				
Yeovil		d 12.32					

Summer 1962 — Up

	M-F	*Q M-F*	*SO*	*SO*	*Q SO*	*SO*
Waterloo	a 3.29	a 3.21	a 3.53	a 4.19	a 5.6	a 5.24
Ilfracombe	d 10.30		d 10.30			
Torrington	d 10.30			d 10.48		
Bude	d 10.20	d 10.20			d 11.45	d 11.45
Padstow	d 9.33	d 9.33				d 11.0
Plymouth	d 10.2	d 10.2				
Yeovil	d 12.32					

Notes on the 'ACE' Times and Schedules

'am' and 'pm' are omitted, as all runs start in the morning and finish in the afternoon.
The time notation is of the period; the practice of describing '2.3pm' as '14.03' came after the 'ACE' ceased to run. **a** arrive **pu** pick up only **d** depart **sd** set down only **x** crosses another train on a single line route **Q** runs when required **o** overtakes another train **–** between times denotes a stop

Table 3

Specimen Schedules

	11 Jul 1926 *M-S* *Down*	**11 Jul 1926** *M-F* *Down*	**11 Jul 1926** *M-S* *Up*	**11 Jul 1926** *M-F* *Up*
Waterloo	d 11.0	d 11.10	a 3.44	a 3.39
Clapham Jn	11.7	11.17	3.36½	3.31
Surbiton		pu 11.28-11.30		3.17-3.19
Hampton Court Jn	11.17½	11.33	3.27	3.14½
Woking		11.45		3.4
Woking Jn	11.29			
Sturt Lane Jn	11.37½	11.55	3.16½	2.57
Basingstoke	11.54	12.12-12.15	2.55½	2.42
Worting Jn	11.57		2.53	2.39½
Andover Jn	12.12	12.30	2.36	2.23
Salisbury	12.30-12.36	12.49-12.55	2.8-2.14	1.54-2.0
Templecombe	1.10	1.29	1.39	
Yeovil Jn	1.21	1.41-1.45	1.27	1.3-1.9
Sidmouth Jn	2.3	2.30	12.48	
Exmouth Jn	2.13	2.40	12.35	12.7
Exeter Queen Street	2.16-2.33	2.43-2.51	12.12-12.32	11.56-12.4
Exeter St David's	2.36-2.39	2.54-2.57	12.5-12.9	11.49-11.53
Cowley Bridge Jn	2.42	3.0	12.2	11.46
Yeoford			11.49-11.50	11.32-11.34
Coleford Jn	2.55		11.47	11.30
Okehampton	3.16-3.20		11.29-11.31	11.9-11.14
Meldon Jn		3.42	11.25	11.5
Tavistock	3.45-3.47		11.0-11.2	
Bere Alston			10.48-10.49	
Devonport K.R.	4.9-4.13		10.29-10.31	
Devonport Jn	4.15		10.28	
Plymouth N.R.	4.16-4.20		10.24-10.26	
Mutley	4.21-4.22		10.22-10.23	
Lipson Jn	4.25		10.19	
Mount Gould Jn	4.26		10.18	
Friary Jn	4.26½		10.17	
Plymouth Friary	a 4.29		d 10.15	
Exeter Queen Street	2.16-2.25		12.23-12.32	
Exeter St David's	2.28-2.31		12.16-12.20	
Cowley Bridge Jn	2.34		12.13	
Yeoford			12.0-12.1	
Coleford Jn	2.48		11.58	
Copplestone	2.52		11.55	
Morchard Road	2.54½		11.51½	
Lapford	2.58		11.47	
Eggesford	x 3.4		11.40½	
South Molton Road	3.10		11.34	
Portsmouth Arms	3.15		11.28	
Umberleigh	x 3.21		11.22	
Barnstaple Jn	3.31-3.37		11.5-11.11	
Barnstaple Town	3.40-3.43		10.59-11.2	
Pottington	3.44		10.58	
Wrafton	3.50-3.51		10.51-10.52	
Braunton	3.53-3.56		10.46-10.49	
Mortehoe	4.11-4.14		10.32-10.35	
Ilfracombe	a 4.24		d 10.22	
Barnstaple Jn	3.31-3.42		10.56-11.1	
Fremington	3.47		10.51	
Instow	3.52-3.54		x 10.42-10.44	
Bideford	3.59-4.3		10.34-10.37	
Torrington	a 4.12		d 10.25	

	11 Jul 1926 *M-S* *Down*	11 Jul 1926 *M-F* *Down*	11 Jul 1926 *M-S* *Up*	11 Jul 1926 *M-F* *Up*
Meldon Jn		3.42		11.5
Ashbury		x 3.50		x 10.52-10.53
Halwill Jn		3.56-4.1		x 10.34-10.43
Ashwater		x 4.9		10.23-10.24
Tower Hill		4.13½		10.15-10.16
Launceston		x 4.20-4.24		10.2-10.7
Egloskerry		4.31½		9.54-9.55
Tresmeer		4.38½		x 9.44-9.48
Otterham		4.48-4.50		9.35-9.37
Camelford		4.58-5.2		9.24-9.27
Delabole		5.7-5.9		9.17-9.18
Port Isaac Road		5.16-5.18		9.6-9.8
St Kew Highway		5.22		8.58-8.59
Wadebridge		5.28-5.32		8.44-8.49
Padstow		a 5.41		d 8.35
Halwill Jn				10.26-10.43
Dunsland Cross				x 10.18-10.19
Holsworthy				10.6-10.9
Whitstone				x 9.56-9.57
Bude				d 9.45
Yeovil Jn		1.41-1.50		12.54-1.9
Axminster		2.20-2.25		12.20-12.26
Seaton Jn		2.31-2.35		12.13-12.15
Honiton		2.51-2.53		12.0-12.2
Sidmouth Jn		3.0-3.7/3.17		11.44-11.52
Sidmouth Jn		3.0-3.7		11.44-11.52
Ottery St Mary		3.12½		x 11.34-11.36
Tipton St John's		x 3.16		x 11.24-11.30
Sidmouth		a 3.24		d 11.15
Sidmouth Jn		3.0-3.17		
Ottery St Mary		x 3.23-3.24		
Tipton St John's		x 3.28-3.30		11.14-11.30
Newton Poppleford				11.9-11.10
East Budleigh		3.37-3.38		11.3-11.4
Budleigh Salterton		3.43-3.47		x 10.55-10.59
Littleham		3.55-3.56		10.45-10.47
Exmouth		a 4.0		d 10.40

	5 Jul 1937 *M-F* *Down*	5 Jul 1937 *M-F* *Up*	27 Sep 1937 *M-S* *Down*	27 Sep 1937 *M-S* *Up*
Waterloo	d11.0	a 3.40	d 11.0	a 3.49
Clapham Jn	11.7	3.33	11.7	3.42
Hampton Court Jn	11.17		11.17	
Woking Jn	11.28	3.14	11.28	3.23
Worting Jn	11.54	2.51	11.54	3.0
Andover Jn				2.44
Salisbury	12.26-12.31	2.8-2.14	12.26-12.31	2.16-2.22
Yeovil Jn	1.14	1.27	1.14	1.35
Sidmouth Jn	1.54-1.58		1.54-1.58	12.47-12.54
Exmouth Jn	2.9	12.33	2.9	12.33
Exeter Central	2.12-2.18	12.12-12.30	2.12-2.25	12.12-12.30
Exeter St David's	2.21-2.24	12.5-12.9	2.28-2.31	12.5½-12.9
Cowley Bridge Jn	2.27	12.2	2.34	12.2½
Newton St Cyres		11.56-11.57		
Crediton		11.50-11.51		
Yeoford		11.42-11.44		11.49½-11.50½

	5 Jul 1937 *M-F* *Down*	5 Jul 1937 *M-F* *Up*	27 Sep 1937 *M-S* *Down*	27 Sep 1937 *M-S* *Up*
Coleford Jn	2.41	11.40	2.48	11.47½
Bow		11.33-11.44		11.41-11.41½
North Tawton		11.26-11.27		
Okehampton	3.2-3.6	11.6-11.14	3.9-3.13	11.24-11.28
Meldon Jn		11.2		11.20
Lydford				pu if Q
Tavistock	3.31-3.32		3.38-3.39	10.56-10.57
Bere Alston				10.43½-10.44½
Devonport K.R.	3.58-4.0		4.5-4.7	10.24-10.26
Devonport Jn	4.2		4.9	10.23
Plymouth N.R.	4.3-4.5		4.10-4.12	10.19-10.21
Mutley				10.17-10.18
Lipson Jn	4.9		4.16	10.14
Mount Gould Jn	4.10		4.17	10.13
Friary Jn	4.10½		4.17½	10.12
Plymouth Friary	a 4.13		a 4.20	d 10.10
Exeter Central		12.24-12.30	2.12-2.18	12.24-12.30
Exeter St David's		12.18-12.21	2.21-2.24	12.18-12.21
Cowley Bridge Jn		12.15	2.27	12.15
Yeoford		12.1-12.3		12.1-12.3
Coleford Jn		11.59	2.41	11.59
Copplestone		11.57	2.44	11.57
Morchard Road		11.54	2.46½	11.54
Lapford		11.50	2.50	11.50
Eggesford		11.44	2.55½	11.44
South Molton Road		x 11.38	3.1	x 11.38
Portsmouth Arms		11.32½-11.33	3.6 sd	11.32½-11.33
Umberleigh		11.25-11.25½	3.11	11.25-11.25½
Barnstaple Jn		11.9-11.14	3.20-3.26	11.9-11.14
Barnstaple Town		11.5-11.6	3.29-3.30	11.5-11.6
Pottington		11.4	3.31	11.4
Braunton		10.55-10.57	3.38-3.39½	10.55-10.57
Mortehoe		10.42-10.45	3.56½-3.58	10.42-10.45
Ilfracombe		d 10.30	a 4.6	d 10.30
Barnstaple Jn		11.0-11.14	3.20-3.30	11.0-11.14
Fremington		10.54-10.55	x 3.35	10.54-10.55
Instow		10.46-10.47	3.40-3.41	10.46-10.47
Bideford		x 10.37-10.41	3.46-3.49	10.37-10.41
Torrington		d 10.28	a 3.58	d 10.28
Okehampton	3.6-3.30	11.6-11.14	3.9-3.30	11.6-11.28
Meldon Jn	3.38	11.2	3.38	11.2
Maddaford Moor	3.42-3.43	10.55-10.56	3.42-3.44	10.55-10.56
Ashbury	x 3.50-3.50½	x 10.45-10.47	3.51-3.51½	x 10.45-10.47
Halwill Jn	3.56½-3.59½	x 10.28-10.36	3.57½-4.1½	10.28-10.36
Ashwater	x 4.6½-4.7½	10.18-10.19	x 4.8½-4.10½	10.18-10.19
Tower Hill	4.13½-4.14½	10.11-10.12	4.16½-4.17	10.11-10.12
Launceston	x 4.21½-4.25	9.59½-10.4	4.25-4.26½	9.59½-10.4
Egloskerry	x 4.32-4.33	9.52-9.53	x 4.34½-4.35½	9.52-9.53
Tresmeer	4.40-4.41	9.44-9.46	4.42½-4.43	9.44-9.46
Otterham	4.50-4.51	x 9.35½-9.37	4.52-4.53	x 9.35½-9.37
Camelford	4.48-4.59	9.25½-9.28½	5.0-5.1	9.25½--9.28½
Delabole	5.4-5.5	9.18-9.20	o 5.6-5.7	9.18-9.20
Port Isaac Road	5.11-5.12	9.8-9.9	x 5.14-5.15	9.8-9.9
St Kew Highway	5.16-5.17	9.1-9.2	x 5.19-5.20	9.1-9.2
Wadebridge	5.23-5.27	x 8.49-8.53	5.27-5.28	8.49-8.53
Padstow	a 5.36	d 8.40	a 5.37	d 8.40

	5 Jul 1937	**5 Jul 1937**	**27 Sep 1937**	**27 Sep 1937**
	M-F	*M-F*	*M-S*	*M-S*
	Down	*Up*	*Down*	*Up*
Halwill Jn	3.56½-4.20	10.20-10.36	3.57½-4.5	x 10.20-10.36
Dunsland Cross	x 4.26-4.26½	10.12-10.13	x 4.11-4.12	10.12-10.13
Holsworthy	4.34½-4.36	o 10.1-10.3	4.20-4.21	o 10.1-10.3
Whitstone	4.44-4.45	x 9.51-9.52	4.29-4.30	x 9.51-9.52
Bude	a 4.54	d 9.40	a 4.39	d 9.40
Axminster	2.32-2.46			
Combpyne	2.58½-2.59			
Lyme Regis	a 3.6			
Seaton Jn	2.41-2.50		2.41-2.50	12.3
Colyton	2.54-2.54½		2.54-2.54½	11.58½-11.59
Colyford	2.57-2.57½		2.57-2.57½	11.54½-11.55
Seaton	a 3.2		a 3.2	d 11.50
Sidmouth Jn			1.54-2.0	12.45-12.54
Ottery St Mary			x 2.5-2.6	12.36-12.37
Tipton St John's			2.10-2.14	12.28-12.32
Sidmouth			a 2.23	d 12.20
Tipton St John's			2.10-2.19	12.19-12.32
Newton Poppleford			2.21½-2.22½	12.15-12.15½
East Budleigh			2.27-2.28	12.9½-12.10
Budleigh Salterton			2.32-2.34	ox 12.3-12.6
Littleham			2.41-2.42	x 11.55-11.56
Exmouth			a 2.46	d 11.50
Salisbury	12.26-12.38	1.59-2.14	12.26-12.38	a 2.0
Wilton	12.44-12.44½		12.44-12.44½	
Dinton	12.53½-12.54		12.53½-12.54	
Tisbury	1.1-1.2		1.1-1.2	
Semley	1.10½-1.11½		1.10½-1.11½	
Gillingham	1.17½-1.19	1.30-1.31	1.17½-1.19	1.32-1.33
Templecombe	1.28½-1.31	1.17-1.20	1.28½-1.31	1.18-1.22
Milborne Port	1.36½-1.37½		1.36½-1.37½	
Sherborne	1.43-1.44	1.4-1.6	1.43-1.44	1.6-1.7
Yeovil Jn	1.51-1.53	12.54-12.56	1.51-1.53	12.56-12.58
Sutton Bingham	1.58-1.58½		1.58-1.58½	
Crewkerne	2.8-2.10½	12.41-12.42	2.8-2.10½	12.42-12.44
Chard Jn	2.23-2.25	12.25-12.27	2.23-2.25	12.26-12.28
Axminster	2.32-2.35	12.12-12.17	2.32-2.35	12.16-12.18
Seaton Jn	2.41-2.45	12.2½-12.7	2.41-2.45	12.7-12.11
Honiton	3.0-3.1	11.50½-11.51½	3.0-3.1	11.55-11.56
Sidmouth Jn	3.7½-3.10	11.42-11.43	3.7½-3.10	11.45-11.47
Whimple		11.34-11.35		11.37-11.38
Broad Clyst				11.29-11.30
Pinhoe		11.24-11.25		11.24-11.25
Exmouth Jn	3.22	11.21	3.22	11.21
Exeter Central	a 3.25	11.12-11.18	a 3.25	11.12-11.18

	1 Jan 1940	**1 Jan 1940**	**15 Sep 1952**	**6 Oct 1947**
	Down	*Up*	*Down*	*Up*
	M-S	*M-S*	*M-F*	*M-S*
Waterloo	d 10.50	a 2.25	d 11.0	a 4.41
Clapham	10.57	2.18	11.7	4.34
Hampton Court Jn	11.8		11.18	4.22
Woking				4.10
Woking Jn	11.21½	1.56	11.28	
Worting Jn	11.52	1.30	11.51	3.45
Salisbury	12.33-12.38	12.38-12.44	12.23-12.28	3.0-3.6

	1 Jan 1940 *Down* *M-S*	1 Jan 1940 *Up* *M-S*	15 Sep 1952 *Down* *M-F*	6 Oct 1947 *Up* *M-S*
Templecombe	1.12	11.57-12.1		2.20-2.23
Sherborne				2.7-2.9
Yeovil Jn	1.25	11.43	1.19	1.57-2.0
Axminster				1.26-1.28
Sidmouth Jn	2.9-2.12	10.48-10.55	1.48-1.52	1.1-1.6
Exmouth Jn	2.25	10.33	2.3	12.45
Exeter Central	2.28-2.45	10.24-10.30	2.6-2.19	12.30-12.42
				[not thru carr]
Exeter Central				12.17-12.25
Exeter St David's	2.48-2.51	10.18-10.21	2.22-2.26	12.8-12.14
Cowley Bridge Jn	2.54	10.13	2.29	12.5
Credition		10.4½-10.5		
Yeoford	3.7-3.8	9.57½-9.58½		11.49-11.51
Coleford Jn	3.10	9.55½	2.43	11.47
North Tawton	3.23-3.24	9.46½-9.47	2.55-2.56	
Okehampton	3.36-3.40	9.35-9.36½	3.8-3.22	11.26-11.30
Meldon Jn		9.31	3.30	11.22
Bridestowe	3.53-3.54			11.13-11.14
Lydford	4.0-4.1	9.16-9.16½		11.5-11.6
Brentor	4.4-4.5			
Tavistock	4.13-4.14	9.2-9.3	3.47-3.48	10.49-10.52
Bere Alston				10.36½-10.37½
Devonport K.R.	4.40-4.43	8.32-8.35	4.14-4.16	10.15-10.19
Devonport Jn	4.45	8.31	4.18	10.14
Plymouth N.R.	4.46-4.49	8.28-8.29	4.20-4.22	10.8-10.12
Lipson Jn	4.53	8.24	4.26	10.4
Mount Gould Jn	4.54	8.23	4.27	10.3
Friary Jn	4.54½	8.22	4.27½	10.2
Plymouth Friary	a 4.57	d 8.20	a 4.30	d 10.0
Exeter Central	2.28-2.35	10.8-10.30	2.6-2.12	12.30-12.42
Exeter St David's	2.38-2.41	10.2-10.5	2.15-2.18	12.22-12.27
Cowley Bridge Jn	2.44	9.59	2.21	12.19
Newton St Cyres				12.13-12.14
Crediton				12.7-12.8
Yeoford				12.0-12.1
Coleford Jn	2.58	9.47	2.35	11.58
Copplestone	3.1	o 9.45	2.38	11.54-11.55
Morchard Road	3.4	9.42	2.40½	11.49-11.50
Lapford	3.7	x 9.36-9.37	2.44	11.43-11.44
Eggesford	3.15	9.29-9.30	2.50-2.51	x 11.36-11.37
South Molton Rd	3.21	x 9.21-9.23	2.57	11.29-11.30
Portsmouth Arms	3.27 sd	9.15 pu	3.2	11.23-11.24
Umberleigh	3.33	9.9 pu	3.7	11.16-11.17
Chapelton				11.10-11.11
Barnstaple Jn	3.43-3.50	8.54-8.59	3.16-3.20	10.58-11.3
Barnstaple Town	3.53-3.54	8.49-8.51	3.23-3.24	10.53-10.55
Pottington	3.55	8.48	3.25	10.52
Wrafton		8.41-8.42	3.31-3.32	10.44-10.46
Braunton	4.2-4.4	8.38-8.39	3.34-3.36	10.39-10.42
Mortehoe	4.21-4.22	8.27-8.28	3.53-3.54	10.27-10.29
Ilfracombe	a 4.30	d 8.15	a 4.2	d 10.15
Barnstaple Jn	3.43-4.0	8.45-8.59	3.16-3.25	10.48-11.3
Fremington	4.5-4.6	8.39-8.40	3.30-3.31	10.42-10.43
Instow	4.12-4.13	x 8.31-8.32	3.37-3.38	10.34-10.35
Bideford	4.18-4.22	8.24-8.26	3.43-3.48	x 10.24-10.29
Torrington	a 4.31	d 8.15	a 3.57	d 10.15

	1 Jan 1940 *Down* *M-S*	1 Jan 1940 *Up* *M-S*	15 Sep 1952 *Down* *M-F*	6 Oct 1947 *Up* *M-S*
Exeter Central				12.5-12.42
Exeter St David's				11.57-12.2
Cowley Bridge Jn				11.54
Crediton				11.42-11.44
Yeoford				11.34-11.36
Coleford Jn				11.32
Bow				11.25-11.26
North Tawton				11.17-11.19
Sampford Courtenay				11.11-11.12
Okehampton	d 3.55	a 9.17	3.8-3.12	11.0-11.5
Meldon Jn	4.4	9.13	3.20	10.56
Maddaford Moor	4.8-4.10	9.6-9.7	3.24-3.25	10.49-10.50
Ashbury	x 4.17-4.20	x 8.58-8.59	x 3.32-3.33	10.40-10.41
Halwill Jn	4.27-4.30	8.46-8.49	3.39-3.43	10.22-10.31
Ashwater	4.37-4.38	8.36-8.37	3.50-3.51	10.12-10.13
Tower Hill	4.44-4.45	8.29-8.30	x 3.57-3.58	10.5-10.6
Launceston	x 4.52-4.55	d 8.22	4.5-4.8	9.49-9.58
Egloskerry	5.2-5.3		4.16-4.17	9.39-9.42
Tresmeer	5.10-5.11		x 4.24-4.25	9.31-9.33
Otterham	5.20-5.21		4.34-4.35	9.22-9.24
Camelford	5.28-5.30		4.42-4.43	x 9.12-9.15
Delabole	ox 5.35-5.37		4.48-4.49	9.5-9.6
Port Isaac Road	5.44-5.45		x 4.56-4.56½	8.55-8.56
St Kew Highway	x 5.49-5.50		5.0½-5.1	8.48-8.49
Wadebridge	x 5.57-6.10		x 5.8-5.12	8.34-8.40
Padstow	a 6.19		a 5.21	d 8.25
Halwill Jn	4.27-4.35	8.41-8.49	3.39-3.47	x 10.15-10.31
Dunsland Cross	4.41-4.42	8.33-8.34	x 3.53-3.54	10.7-10.8
Holsworthy	4.50-4.51	8.23-8.24	x 4.2-4.3	9.56-9.57
Whitstone	4.59-5.0	8.13-8.14	4.11-4.12	9.46-9.47
Bude	a 5.9	d 8.2	a 4.21	d 9.35
Seaton Jn			2.37-3.15	
Colyton			3.19-3.19½	
Colyford			3.22-3.22½	
Seaton			a 3.27	
Sidmouth Jn			1.48-1.56	
Ottery St Mary			2.1-2.2	
Tipton St John's			x 2.6-2.10	
Sidmouth			a 2.19	
Tipton St John's			2.6-2.16	
Newton Poppleford			2.18½-2.19½	
East Budleigh			2.24-2.25	
Budleigh Salterton			2.29-2.31	
Littleham			2.38-2.39	
Exmouth			a 2.43	
Salisbury			12.23-12.36	
Wilton			12.42-12.42½	
Dinton			12.51½-12.52	
Tisbury			12.59-1.0	
Semley			1.8½- 1.9½	
Gillingham			1.15½-1.17	
Templecombe			1.26½-1.29	
Milborne Port			1.34½-1.35	
Sherborne			1.41½-1.42	
Yeovil Jn			1.49-1.56	
Crewkerne			2.8-2.10	

	1 Jan 1940 *Down* *M-S*	1 Jan 1940 *Up* *M-S*	15 Sep 1952 *Down* *M-F*	6 Oct 1947 *Up* *M-S*
Chard Jn			2.20½-2.22½	
Axminster			2.29-2.32	
Seaton Jn			2.37-2.39	
Honiton			2.51-2.52	
Sidmouth Jn			2.57½-3.0	
Whimple			3.5-3.6	
Broad Clyst			3.11-3.11½	
Pinhoe			3.15½-3.16	
Exmouth Jn			3.20	
Exeter Central			a 3.23	

	18 Jun 1962 *M-F* *Down*	18 Jun 1962 *M-F Q* *Down*	18 Jun 1962 *M-F* *Up*	18 Jun 1962 *M-F* *Up*
Waterloo	d 11.0	d 11.5	a 3.21	a 3.29
Clapham Jn	11.7	11.12	3.14	3.22
Hampton Court Jn	11.18	11.23	3.4	
Woking Jn	11.27	11.36	2.53	3.3
Worting Jn	11.50	11.59	2.33	2.43
Salisbury	12.20-12.25	12.29½-12.34	1.53-1.59	2.3-2.9
Yeovil Jn	1.5	1.14	1.13	1.26
Axminster		1.36-1.37		
Sidmouth Jn	1.40-1.44			12.47-12.49
Exmouth Jn	1.55	2.6		
Exeter Central	1.58-2.15	2.9-2.15	12.12-12.18	12.12-12.30
Exeter St David's	2.18-2.21		12.5-12.9	12.5-12.9
Cowley Bridge Jn	2.24		12.2	12.2
Yeoford			11.49-11.50	11.49-11.50
Coleford Jn	2.38		11.47	11.47
North Tawton	2.49-2.50			
Okehampton	3.2-3.16		11.14-11.31	11.14-11.31
Meldon Jn	3.24		11.10	11.10
Bridestowe	3.29-3.29½		11.1½-11.2	11.1½-11.2
Lydford	3.35½-3.36		10.54-10.54½	10.54-10.54½
Tavistock	3.47½-3.48½		10.40-10.41	10.40-10.41
Bere Alston			10.27-10.28½	10.27-10.28½
St Budeaux			10.12-10.13	10.12-10.13
Devonport K.R.	4.14-4.18		10.5-10.7	10.5-10.7
Devonport Jn	4.20		10.4	10.4
Plymouth N.R.	4.22-4.33ecs		ecs9.52-10.2	ecs9.52-10.2
Lipson Jn	4.37		9.48	9.48
Mount Gould Jn	a 4.40		d 9.44ecs	d 9.44ecs
Exeter Central	1.58-2.4			12.24-12.30
Exeter St David's	2.7-2.11			12.17-12.21
Cowley Bridge Jn	2.14			12.14
Yeoford				12.1-12.2
Coleford Jn	2.28			11.59
Copplestone	2.31			11.56
Morchard Road	2.33½			11.54
Lapford	2.37			x 11.51
Eggesford	2.43-2.44			11.44-11.45
King's Nympton	2.50			11.38
Portsmouth Arms	2.55			11.33
Umberleigh	3.0			11.28
Barnstaple Jn	3.9-3.13			11.13-11.18
Barnstaple Town	3.16-3.17			11.8-11.10
Pottington	3.18			11.7
Wrafton	3.24-3.25			10.59-11.1
Braunton	3.27-3.29			10.53-10.57

	18 Jun 1962 *M-F* *Down*	18 Jun 1962 *M-FQ* *Down*	18 Jun 1962 *M-F* *Up*	18 Jun 1962 *M-F* *Up*
Mortehoe	3.46-3.47			10.42-10.44
Ilfracombe	a 3.55			d 10.30
Barnstaple Jn	3.9-3.18			11.3-11.18
Fremington	x 3.23-3.24			10.57-10.58
Instow	3.30-3.31			10.49-10.50
Bideford	3.36-3.39			x 10.40-10.44
Torrington	a 3.49			d 10.30
		After 10 Sep		
Okehampton	3.2-3.8	3.2-3.8	11.27-11.31	10.57-11.19
Meldon Jn	3.16	3.16	11.23	10.53
Maddaford Moor				10.46-10.47
Ashbury	3.24	3.26-3.27	11.14	10.37-10.38
Halwill Jn	3.30-3.33	3.33-3.37	11.2-11.16	x 10.22-10.28
Ashwater	3.39	3.44-3.45	10.54	10.12-10.13
Tower Hill	3.44	3.51-3.52	x 10.48	10.5-10.6
Launceston	3.50-3.53	3.59-4.4	10.37-10.41	9.54-9.58
Egloskerry	4.0	4.12-4.13	10.30½	9.46-9.47
Tresmeer	4.7	x 4.20-4.24	10.25	9.39-9.40
Otterham	x 4.16-4.17	4.33-4.34	10.17-10.18	x 9.31-9.32
Camelford	4.24-4.25	4.41-4.42	x 10.9-10.10	9.22-9.24
Delabole	4.30-4.31	4.47-4.48	10.4-10.5	9.15-9.16
Port Isaac Road	4.38-4.39	x 4.55-4.55½	9.55-9.56	9.5-9.6
St Kew Highway	4.43	4.59½-5.0	9.50½	x 8.54-8.59
Wadebridge	4.49-4.51	x 5.7-5.12	9.42-9.44	x 8.39-8.46
Padstow	a 5.0	a 5.21	d 9.33	d 8.30
		After 10 Sep		
Halwill Jn	3.30-3.37	3.33-3.41	10.54-11.6	10.10-10.22
Dunsland Cross	x 3.43-3.44	x 3.47-3.49	x 10.47	10.2-10.3
Holsworthy	x 3.52-3.54	x 3.57-3.58	10.38-10.40	x 9.51-9.53
Whitstone	4.2-4.3	4.6-4.7	x 10.30	9.41-9.42
Bude	a 4.12	a 4.16	d 10.20	d 9.30
Sidmouth Jn	1.40-1.45	Yeovil Jn	12.36-12.46	
Ottery St Mary	1.50-1.51	Yeovil Town	d 12.32	
Tipton St John's	1.55-1.58			
Sidmouth	a 2.6			
Tipton St John's	1.55-2.2			
Newton Poppleford	2.4½-2.5½			
East Budleigh	2.10-2.10½			
Budleigh Salterton	2.14½-2.15½			
Littleham	2.22½-2.23			
Exmouth	a 2.17			
Salisbury	12.20-12.36		1.49-1.59	
Wilton	12.42-12.42½			
Dinton	12.51½-12.52			
Tisbury	12.59-1.0			
Semley	1.8½-1.9½			
Gillingham	1.15½-1.17		1.22-1.24	
Templecombe	1.26½-1.29		1.10-1.13	
Milborne Port	1.34½-1.35		1.4½-1.5	
Sherborne	1.41½-1.42		12.53-12.57	
Yeovil Jn	1.49-1.56		12.38-12.46	
Crewkerne	2.8-2.10		12.25½-12.27	
Chard Jn	2.20½-2.22½		12.12-12.14	
Axminster	2.29-2.32		12.2-12.4	
Seaton Jn	2.37-2.39		11.55-11.57	

After 10 Sep *cont.*				
	Down	*Up*	*Down*	*Up*
	M-S	*M-S*	*M-F*	*M-S*
Honiton	2.51-2.52		11.44½-11.45½	
Sidmouth Jn	2.57½-3.0		11.36-11.37	
Whimple	3.5-3.6		11.29-11.29½	
Broad Clyst	3.11-3.11½		11.22-11.22½	
Pinhoe	3.15½-3.16		11.18-11.18½	
Exmouth Jn	3.20		11.15	
Exeter Central	a 3.23		d 11.12	
	10 min later until 10 Sep			

Above: Waterloo station, viewed from the Shell Co office building. The lower roof in front is the Windsor station, completed in 1885, the rest being the 1922 station. The cloud on the far right comes from two steam trains, a departure in Platform 11 and one running into Platform 12. Beyond are 'fast' and 'semi-fast' Portsmouth electric trains. *B. Wright/MNLPS Collection*

Left: On 22 September 1962 the down winter 'ACE', the BR Standard three-set for Ilfracombe followed by a string of Bulleid Brake Composites, sets out from London. The driver of No 35029 *Ellerman Lines* leans from his side window to get a sight through the curve of Vauxhall station as he passes signal WA3, the up Main Local starter. *R.L. Sewell*

3

The Route

The Southampton and London Railway and Dock Co was the first to commence design of a really long railway route, and indeed was in 1831 by far the biggest engineering project in the world, so it is not surprising that it faltered at first, and other projects started later were finished sooner. It opened from Nine Elms to Woking on 21 May 1838. This opening was rushed through in order to carry people to Surbiton for the Epsom Races, thus setting the precedent for passenger and leisure travel which has characterised the line ever since. Onward construction to Basingstoke was completed on 10 June 1839, and the eastern end was extended to Waterloo Bridge on 11 July 1848.

As the London and South Western Railway, it completed a route to Salisbury on 1 May 1857, and from Yeovil to Exeter on 19 July 1860. The Salisbury and Yeovil, opened on 1 June 1860, was an independent company, and was the most successful railway company ever; its dividends reached the fantastic figure of 14% before it was bought out by the LSWR. Exeter Queen Street station was a terminus until 1 February 1862, when the incline to St David's was opened to connect with the LSWR's acquisitions in Devon.

The Exeter and Crediton Railway, then a broad gauge line leased to the Bristol and Exeter Railway, was opened on 12 May 1851, and was continued by the North Devon Railway to Fremington on 1 August 1854 and Bideford on 1 November 1855. The LSWR took over the lease from 1 February 1862 and began running narrow gauge trains the next year; the extension to Torrington was completed on 24 July 1872. The Ilfracombe line, promoted by a nominally independent company with LSWR support, was opened on 20 July 1874 after four years' struggle with the terrain and a far longer tussle between groups of rival promoters.

Westwards from Coleford Junction, an Okehampton Railway Company, with illicit LSWR backing, was incorporated in 1862 and obtained powers to extend to Lydford, whence the Launceston and South Devon Railway would give access to Plymouth. It was not until 12 October 1874 that the trains began running the full distance, and two years later that they entered a new terminus at Devonport King's Road. As from 2 June 1890 the Plymouth, Devonport and South Western Junction Railway provided an independent route from Lydford to Devonport.

In 1873 a branch from Okehampton to Holsworthy was authorised, opening on 18 January 1879. The LSWR eventually succeeded in completing the extension to Bude on 10 August 1898. The North Cornwall Railway, an independent company although worked by the LSWR, began work on its line in 1882, but it was not until 1 June 1895 that its trains ran into Wadebridge, and December 1896 that work began on the last piece towards Padstow. That was opened on 23 March 1899.

The east Devon branches with which we are concerned were all built by locally run and funded companies, the great main line having looked at them most off-handedly until condescending to buy them out after a few years. Seaton opened on 16 March 1868, Sidmouth on 6 July 1874, Budleigh Salterton on 15 May 1897, Budleigh–Exmouth (built by the LSWR) on 1 June 1903, and Lyme Regis, the last part of the 'ACE' network to come into being, on 24 August 1903. Finally, there is the short branch from Yeovil Junction to Yeovil Town, which fed a coach into the up train in postwar years. This was the end part of the Salisbury and Yeovil main line as originally built.

The above summary is just to give the basic dates; many books are available, detailing the full history of the political and financial intrigues of the railway promoters, and pretty sordid most of it was.

After 1926, although there was no major change, a great deal of work was done enlarging stations, strengthening the track and improving signalling. The biggest single such scheme was the resignalling of Waterloo to Hampton Court Junction, carried out in 1936. With the removal of Waterloo A Signalbox, which spanned the tracks above Westminster Bridge Road, it drastically changed the outlook on this gateway to the west.

Another modernisation as far as Woking Junction took place during 1938.

The contrast from one end of the route to the other was extreme. The eastern end was the most intensively used surface railway anywhere in the world, and was accordingly complex. Eight running lines were provided from Waterloo to Clapham Junction, at which point there was a spread of 18 tracks. From north to south these were: down Kensington, up Kensington, up Windsor local, up Windsor through, down Windsor through, down Windsor local, No 6 Siding (the exit from Clapham carriage depot), No 2 Siding, No 1 Siding (depot entrance), up main through, down main through, up main local, down main local, exchange siding, and the four tracks of the Brighton line. (Note that the Southern did not have 'fast' or 'slow' lines.)

From Clapham Junction to Worting Junction the main line had four tracks. From Worting, where the Southampton and Salisbury routes diverged, to Plymouth Friary there was a

Above: A down 'ACE' racing through Andover Junction in September 1962. 'MN' No 35015 *Rotterdam Lloyd* is in blue livery and the coaches are in red and cream. *B.E. Coates*

Left: A recent view, 5 September 1993, of an old friend and landmark, the Cowley Bridge Inn, adjoining the junction. *SHA*

double-track line. There was also a double track from Coleford Junction to Copplestone, Umberleigh to Barnstaple Junction and Pottington to Ilfracombe. The rest of the routes, from Copplestone to Umberleigh, Barnstaple Junction to Torrington, Meldon Junction to Bude, Halwill to Padstow and the East Devon branches, comprised single tracks.

Control of trains on the line was conducted in most parts by conventional mechanical signalling systems. On the main line from Waterloo to Basingstoke, and at Grateley and Salisbury, points and signals were power-operated by compressed air, with mechanical and later electrical interlocking systems. There are many little characteristics which go to make one scene different from another, and from the west end of Salisbury platforms the hiss and click of the point machines briskly punctuated the smart pace of the shunting. By the end of steam haulage the air installations from Waterloo to Woking Junction had been replaced by all-electric signalling.

On the single lines the standard method of protection was the Tyer electric tablet system. In BR days the line from Copplestone to Torrington was equipped with the Electric Key Token system. This was the device preferred by the Western Region, which took control of the civil engineering in 1953, and it was also brought in between Ashbury and Halwill, and Holsworthy and Bude. In a programme completed in 1960, single line safety was enhanced by adding the W.R. Sykes & Co system of interlocks between the signals and the tablet instruments.

A Run Down the Line

What made the South Western such a pleasant main line from the passenger's window, and so unprofitable for the proprietors, was the absence of heavy industry. After a train had passed the mess of factories lining the River Wandle near Wimbledon, the major industrial units flanking the railway were so few that they can be listed: the railway's own electricity generating plant at Durnsford Road, the Vickers Aircraft factory at Weybridge, James Walker's Lion Works (producers of the gaskets and gland packings in our locomotives) at Woking, Portal's Overton paper works, McDougall's Andover Flour Mills, the Wiltshire United Dairies plant at Chard Junction, a brush factory and textile machine factory at Axminster, Whiteway's cider factory at Whimple, the Poltimore Brick Works, and then we were in Exeter and passing the Southern's concrete prefabrication works at Exmouth Junction.

The continuous viaduct from Waterloo to Battersea gave the traveller views of the urban scenery, although it was not particularly inspiring before being battered by the Luftwaffe, and in parts positively inhuman after redevelopment. It is quite true that you could see all four sides of the Palace of Westminster clock, the first from the edge of Waterloo Platform 21 and the last in the distance when approaching Clapham Junction. As the train accelerated, from the 40mph speed limit, into Clapham Cutting, green slopes and trees formed the prospect. Suburban houses and factories again formed the view as it crossed the River Wandle, on the east bank of which ran the Surrey Iron Railway, the first public railway in the world. After passing under the Hampton Court Junction flyover, a rural view opened out across the Mole valley and Sandown Park racecourse. The line rose steadily through another deep cutting and across the Wey valley, passing along the northern boundary of Brooklands race track, to Woking. Here the divergence of the Portsmouth line was on a flat junction, although a flyover was sorely needed, for hold-ups were frequent. The summit of the long rise was finally reached at Deepcut, 31 miles from Waterloo. The spot was marked by a very high bridge carrying a road and to its west a squat, massive structure carrying the Basingstoke Canal. The engine would be worked hard up to here but the slight descent into the pine woods of Pirbright helped to bring the speed up to a full gallop, which lasted to Basingstoke. In the yard at Farnborough you might glimpse *Invincible*, the little tank engine which worked traffic down the long siding to the Royal Aircraft Establishment a mile away.

The first 50 miles from London were superbly engineered, nearly straight for the most part and easily graded, and could have been used as a speedway for the fastest trains in the country. However, instead of turning it over to a few flyers, the Southern preferred to develop fast, frequent services for all its stations, large and small.

At Battledown Farm the westward route curved to the right under a flyover carrying the up Bournemouth line and continued on a gradual rise, now through chalk downland scenery, to Oakley. It ran above the River Test as far as Hurstbourne, where the first high viaduct was, then cut across the high ground of Harewood Forest to descend to Andover Junction. All these stations were about a mile from the places they served, Andover presenting a charming view below and to the left. Later, the area between the town and the station was built over. The Midland & South Western Junction line to Cheltenham ran parallel to Red Post Junction, whence it was a steep pull up to Grateley. Near the summit was a little-known flyover junction, the branch to Amesbury and Bulford Camp. This was sheep country, the downs being grassland until during the war much of it was put under corn crops. The land to the south of the line was a Restricted Area surrounding a War Office establishment.

The name of Porton had a sinister ring to a generation of travellers, although it was not until many years after the war that the authorities admitted that it would have produced poison gas to repel the invasion that never came. As the train was speeding down past Porton Down, the spire of Salisbury Cathedral would come into view in the distance, with the older landmarks of Sarum Castle to the right and Figsbury Ring to the left. At this point gravity would be the motive power, with the engine shut down to drifting steam, whereas in the up direction the 10-mile pull from a standing start at Salisbury was considered to be a definitive test of locomotive performance. Finally the train crossed the River Bourne at St Thomas's bridge, the brakes went on and it entered the first tunnel from London, Fisherton. Emerging into the town of Salisbury, it was a slow run round the sharp curves before stopping in the station.

Salisbury was one of those places that swung between peace and hectic activity, for it formed a cross between two passenger services, the West of England and the South Coast–Bristol. Trains in both directions on both routes were timed to be in at the same time to make connections. When that happened, all four lines through the station were occupied and if the shunting was not perfectly organised, a major tangle could result.

The exit from Salisbury seemed leisurely to the passenger, the engine plugging away up a 1 in 115 gradient, mostly in cutting. Another double-track line, the Great Western to Westbury, paralleled it as far as Wilton, where it followed the River Wylye while we turned left to follow the Nadder. The views from the train along here were the very epitome of rural England at its most tranquil and beautiful — and still are, for towns such as Tisbury have survived so far unspoilt.

Hereabouts the engine would be heard working very hard, for the gradient steepened and we were on the roller-coaster profile for which this route was celebrated. The tower of Semley church appeared on the left, the train rounded a curve and headed into a cutting which marked 100 miles from Waterloo. Labouring now, it was another mile to Semley station, where the coaches followed the engine in a nosedive onto a 1 in 100 downhill.

With a prolonged surge of speed we descended to the River Stour, shot through Gillingham and up the other side to Buckhorn Weston Tunnel piercing the ridge on which stood Sandley House. In the cutting just east of the tunnel there was an even more abrupt switch from 1 in 100 up to 1 in 100 down, and then came another swoop across the Blackmoor Vale. Halfway up the other side lay Templecombe, junction with the Somerset and Dorset line which ran along the vale. The next peak was at a little bridge near the village of Stowell. Heading downhill again, we passed Milborne Port station. A port is strictly a place where goods are exchanged; it need not be a seaport, and Milborne Port is an inland market town. The station is some way from it, near a hamlet called Milborne Wick, a few houses, a farm and a watermill which could be seen on the right.

From pasture to meadowland, Sherborne Castle appeared among trees on the left, briefly glimpsed as the train went through the neat stone-built station very fast indeed, and ran along by the River Yeo to Yeovil Junction. This lay in the parish of Clifton Maybank, from which the Great Western took the name for its station alongside the LSWR one. Because it provided the London service for Yeovil, by far the biggest town in south Somerset, it remained an important station even in post-modern years. A couple of miles further on was Sutton Bingham, station for the Cokers, little used and the first on the route to be closed. After closure a reservoir was built right by the site, which made an attraction which might have brought some passengers.

The train went uphill to another peak between Abbot's Hill and Kit Hill, then down to a valley between the Perrotts where the stream is the infant River Parrett. Then came the heaviest climb yet, three miles at 1 in 80 past Crewkerne station and through a short tunnel. Here the line joins the River Axe, which though it rises in the same hillside as the Parrett flows south instead of north. The river was realigned in places to allow the railway a long downhill run, comparable with any such racing stretch in the country apart from the presence of a curve half-way down at Chard Junction, and one where national or even world speed records might have been made, if the Southern Railway had not been concerned with the overall operating picture and kept its track standards to accord with an overall speed limit of 85mph. At the bottom by the village of Whitford, passengers might imagine they could see the sea, but this was not the case, and the first 'ACE' travellers to glimpse salt water were those arriving at Lyme Regis.

The long tunnel under Honiton Hill was reached by long ascents at 1 in 80 from the east and 1 in 100 from the west; a down train emerged from the tunnel high above the River Otter to coast through Honiton. Here a Devonshire motif entered the scenery in the spring: apple blossom. The patron of the orchards was the Whiteway's cider factory at Whimple. The switchback nature of the route continued on a smaller scale with dips into the Otter and Tale valleys and a final long descent to the River Clyst. As the train topped the last rise to Pinhoe, it ran into a built-up area for the first time since leaving Salisbury.

The branch line connections along this stretch were notable for their inconvenient layouts. At Chard Junction the branch had a separate

Above: A sunny day at Okehampton, 7 July 1961. With eight on, No 34033 *Chard* coasts past the outer down home signal. In the left background is the East Okement Viaduct. *Dr T. Gough*

station, connected only via the goods yard headshunt. The Lyme Regis branch dropped into Axminster on a 1 in 80 gradient from Trinity Hill and was connected by a back-shunt into the up siding, which moreover had a public footpath across the middle of it, so any train left standing in it had to be divided and a 20ft gap left. To transfer a coach from the down main to the branch bay entailed three reversals. The Seaton train had to reverse in and out of Seaton Junction station before a platform was provided on the branch line. Sidmouth Junction was rather better, but here again an absence of facing connections, very commendable from the safety aspect, meant that movements onto the branch could only be made by reversing. Given these obstacle courses, the working of through coaches was remarkably expeditious, but that elaborate ritual which so delights railway enthusiasts does not appeal to most passengers and was the reverse of the dog on its hind legs; it was done well, but it should not have been done at all.

After the interlude at Exeter Central your train eased away down the 1 in 37 incline, from the confines of cutting and tunnel to a sudden wide-open view across the River Exe. On the ascent here, even the quiet-voiced 'West Country' would be heard as it lifted you slowly out of the valley. At St David's on the riverbank, Southern trains used the middle platform; the down Southern line led only into the up middle road, while the up Southern was reached only from the down middle and down main. At the north end these three were connected to a short siding for the banking engines.

Thus far, the scenery at least may be glimpsed from the air-conditioned cocoon of a train at the end of the 20th century. Now, however, for the restart from St David's over Red Cow Crossing, the reader must think back to the pre-1964 railway. Settle in a Bulleid coach with the window open to the scented air, the sounds and smells of a live steam engine and the reassuring sights of signalmen standing watch over our progress.

At Cowley Bridge the Plymouth or North Cornwall train sets out on a 27-mile climb to Dartmoor. At first it is gentle enough, the scene pastoral; the junction station of Yeoford where much shunting goes on is in farmland which the motorist penetrates only on twisting, hedge-girt lanes. From Coleford box the Plymouth train pulls away on a rising left-hand curve, leaving the main road and the similar towns of Bow and North Tawton below to its right. The view to the north opens out until in clear weather the heights of Exmoor can be seen over 20 miles away. To the south the ground mounts higher. As we clear the

Left: The Tavy Viaduct; a view from the south end on 3 July 1995. *SHA*

sheltered setting of Sampford Courtenay station the treeless heights of Dartmoor proper come into view. A deep wooded combe appears below; this is the East Okement River, and we take to a ledge on the hillside. What looks like the highest peak is indeed just that, Yes Tor. It is the end of a half-mile-long ridge at whose other end, out of sight, is a rock, High Willhays, which at 2,039ft is actually the highest point on the moor. Here we pull into Okehampton station, fearfully exposed above the town.

The train continues upwards along the edge of the moor until Meldon Quarry appears above it. The engine pants up a shallow cutting to the open plateau where the quarry sidings and buildings lie on the left, and is immediately launched into space — Meldon Viaduct, with the West Okement tumbling far beneath. Through a rocky defile, past Meldon Junction (the box is 200 miles from London) and into another cutting, and this is the summit at 950ft. The next 24½ miles take us very nearly to sea level, at an average gradient of 1 in 144. It is not quite possible to coast all the way, but nearly so.

The once-important town of Lydford is passed without a station. The tourist attraction, Lydford Gorge, starts beneath the viaduct and extends for over a mile, close to the line but hidden under trees, to Lydford Junction station. From this point the Southern and Great Western lines share a narrow valley with the River Burn, until the latter route diverges left and below to enter the south side of Tavistock, while we remain at the high level to the north of the town. It is a punishing uphill hike to catch a Southern train here.

Off the end of Tavistock platforms is a viaduct leading directly into a tunnel and out through more heavy engineering works to sustain the even gradient. Bere Alston and Bere Ferrers are two towns which retain a flavour of what Devon was like before the age of mass mobility, because they are on an isolated strip of land between the rivers Tamar and Tavy — there is no main road bridge over river, either below the Tavistock-Gunnislake

Left: The rural station of Otterham, over 800ft up on the Cornish moors, on 5 July 1961. All the North Cornwall stations had the same design of station house, corrugated-iron lamp room and store, and signalbox. On the right are two permanent way trolley garages. The train is the up Padstow 'ACE' hauled by No 34011 *Tavistock*. *Dr T. Gough*

Right: With just four weeks to go to the end for the through West of England services, Waterloo is as busy as ever. No 34096 *Trevone* looks out from Platform 10; another 'West Country' is pulling away from Platform 8, and a BR Standard engine is approaching on the up main through line to run in to the nearest platform road, No 11. *M. Welch/MNLPS Collection*

Right: No 35017 *Belgian Marine* cruising down towards Basingstoke with the 4pm Waterloo–Exeter on 24 June 1956. *R.C. Riley*

Right: At the end of the four-track line, approaching Worting signalbox, is No 35014 *Nederland Line* with the down train on 14 July 1962. The formation is: 3-set Ilfracombe, Torrington, restaurant set, Padstow, Bude, Plymouth, Exmouth, Sidmouth, Exeter. *F.W. Paige/MNLPS Collection*

road. The way the railway builders found a route through this hilly country is amazing. There is no straight track between Tavistock and Ernesettle on the outskirts of Plymouth. The Tamar appears far below to our right and broadens as we come down to it, until we reach the very tip of the land. In summer it can look beautiful, but at low tide on a dull day with acres of mud in prospect, the rare tourist who penetrates this far feels he has come to the end of the world. The train escapes from it by means of a grand and fitting structure, the 493yd-long Tavy Bridge. Tamerton Foliot station on the far side is also isolated at the end of a promontory between the Tavy and Tamerton Creek. Another bridge takes us across the latter.

One of the most beautiful sights of nature complemented by human ingenuity greets us here, the Royal Albert Bridge striding high above us. It is to be hoped that our fireman has not allowed his fire to run down too much, for we now embark on a 1 in 75 uphill on a continuous curve, passing beneath the GW line again and coming up to its level at the twin St Budeaux stations, Victoria Road and Ferry Road. The Southern then curves round Weston Mill Lake and dives into Ford Tunnel to cross under the GW yet again. At this point both lines are in tunnels, a situation most unusual outside London, and the impression that we are on the Inner Circle is enhanced by the setting of Albert Road Halt between two tunnels. After a stop at the dignified station of Devonport King's Road, we pull up onto Western metals to pass through North Road, which was built for and financed by the LSWR, as all GWR trains in those days went into Millbay. Finally the 'ACE' traverses a half-circle past the back of Laira Yard, to pull up in the urban backwater that is Plymouth Friary.

A North Devon train carries on from Yeoford through rich farming country, mostly dairy, as exemplified by the Ambrosia milk products factory beside Lapford station. The line is straight and easily graded and could have been a high-speed main line were it not for the infamous agreement of 1910, in which the LSWR promised not to improve the line if the Great Western did not improve its Taunton-Barnstaple line. Not until Lapford is past does the valley of the River Yeo close in (there are a lot of rivers Yeo in these parts) and join that of the River Taw, which we follow to its mouth. The whole 25 miles from Copplestone is downhill. A pass of sorts is negotiated through Eggesford, whose station is so close by a mill leat that the down platform backs onto the water. This area is thickly wooded. More water meadows follow, bringing us to Barnstaple Junction.

The Taw valley is still comparatively narrow at this point and the station site is cut away from a hillside, its goods yard extending across to the river. Ilfracombe-bound, we move slowly round a long curve which comes out by Shapland & Petter's works, right by the southern end of Barnstaple's 13th-century bridge. Here the curve reverses onto the iron railway viaduct. It takes up a position on the water's edge, past Town station and a pleasant wooded corner and — yes, it's another River Yeo. A mile further on, a flat expanse beside the estuary is occupied by the RAF's Chivenor airfield, and the railway turns right to enter Braunton. Here, on a Saturday, another engine will be found in one of the short lay-by sidings and there is a pause while it moves onto the rear of our train and is coupled up. Then both engines are put to the bank. First at 1 in 96, then 1 in 80, up the wooded valley to Heddon Mill, then 1 in 40, round the curve past the Foxhunters Inn, panting up to Mortehoe station. The village lies 2 miles away on a headland, well named Mortehoe, for it is fatal to any ship driven onto its cliffs. When the bank engine has uncoupled, we ease away over the summit. If the passenger feels impatient at the maximum speed of 25mph, a view forward would cure that; a winding ledge high above the Slade valley reservoirs, a ramp with apparently nothing ahead of it except the distant sea. Pulling up in the eyrie of Ilfracombe station, only on going out into the forecourt do you discover the town and harbour below.

The run to Torrington is a contrast to the mountaineering needed to gain Ilfracombe. Over the flat salt marshes to Fremington Harbour, it follows the shore line round to the River Torridge. Here it passes one of the very few sites of modern industrial development on the route, East Yelland generating station. This was a product of postwar unification, in this case of the electricity supply; it replaced a piecemeal network of local plants in North Devon, and worked from 1953 until 1984, when it was in turn abandoned in favour of still more centralisation. It received its coal by sea. Instow and Bideford Goods are also on quaysides, and through the life of the 'ACE' were busy with commercial shipping. In the

Right: Battledown Flyover on 4 August 1951. No 30450 *Sir Kay* is wheeling an express through, thought to be the 8am from Ilfracombe and Torrington. The number 262 is a train reporting number, used to enable signalmen to identify the trains on busy days such as summer Saturdays. *E.D. Bruton*

Below right: A view from the A30 bridge west of Salisbury on 3 August 1964. No 35014 *Nederland Line* is accelerating away with the 11am down, the visible coaches being a five-set for Ilfracombe and a restaurant set. Salisbury Cathedral shows dimly through the smoke, as does the GW line which passes out of sight between the bank and the pub on the left. *R.L. Sewell*

262

HERS
ES & STOUT

village of East-the-Water we gain a little height to reach Bideford passenger station, then continue on the level, with pastoral views, to cross the river at Landcross. A short, sharp climb through Landcross Tunnel, then back to the riverside. We cross it three times more before arriving at Torrington station, out of sight of its town but in this case as far below it as Ilfracombe's station is above it.

A Padstow/Bude line train does not quite reach Meldon summit but turns sharp right at the junction onto Maddaford Moor, a conveniently placed ridge of high ground separating two main river systems, the Tamar to the left and the Torridge to the right. It falls away northwards at 1 in 78. That is the ruling gradient (ie the steepest applied in any appreciable length) between Okehampton and Holsworthy; the ruling gradient for the North Cornwall line and the Bude extension is 1 in 73. This is a very open piece of country and it takes very balmy weather indeed to make it feel hospitable. Often it is through a pall of rain that Halwill Junction comes into view, a village brought into being by the railway junction.

Originally the main line but later regarded as the branch, the Bude line continues its descent from the ridge to Holsworthy. Here the station is actually in the town, rare for a British railway; the town lies where a tributary runs into the River Deer, and the position of the station between these two necessitates two major viaducts across them. The eastern one is built in the normal way in stone, but the western one, built in 1897–98, is a remarkable and impressive work made of concrete blocks, as is the smaller viaduct at Woolston further west. This unique construction is a precursor of the modern method of pouring concrete structures *in situ*. A rock cutting near Whitstone station (at Merrifield) brings us into Cornwall and the valley of the River Neet. Bude station lies at the foot of another steep descent, outside the town on low-lying ground near the river — although nearer the Atlantic than any other station, still a good half-mile from the sea.

Above: At around 4pm on 1 September 1958 at Sidmouth Junction, with a backdrop of Cheriton Hill. The 11.30am Brighton-Plymouth through train, hauled by No 34030 *Watersmeet*, is passing at full speed. 'S15' No 30827 at the head of a ballast train waits on the up siding. *K.L. Cook*

Departing from Halwill on the North Cornwall Railway (never part of the LSWR but independent until coerced into the Southern Group) entails one of those curves that when seen from on board the train seem to go on for ever. (Following a spectacular runaway of a goods train from this curve, a rule was made that trains were not to be divided on it but shunted onto the Bude line instead.) It brings us into the upper part of a very peaceful and beautiful valley, of the River Carey. The sublime beauty of this route is in no small measure due to the circumstance that it is nowhere accompanied by a main road. We run downhill at the ruling gradient to the Tamar at Polson Bridge, where we leave England and enter Cornwall. This boundary is in practical terms a very real one; there are only three road bridges over the Tamar below Polson, plus Calstock and Saltash railway crossings. Consequently, although the two railway bridges here may slumber in the sun, the winding road up into the neat little town of Launceston is a day-long traffic jam all summer as lorries toil noisily and odorously up the valley sides.

Two railways, ours and the GW line coming up from Lifton, head across the Tamar into another side valley, the River Kensey. A mile upstream the two stations of Launceston nestle

Right: The first portion of the 11am down, bound for Plymouth, eases down the incline from Exeter Central: engine No 34034 *Honiton*. On the siding above, the crew of No 34058 *Sir Frederick Pile* are ready for the tip to back onto the Padstow/Bude portion. Both these engines were rebuilt in 1960. *S. Creer*

Centre right: An unusual view of the Exeter incline, on 14 June 1957. The train descending is the second, Ilfracombe/Torrington, portion of the 11am down, but since this is a Sunday it is not an 'ACE'. The engine is No 34072 *257 Squadron*, now preserved for posterity. *M. Mensing*

Below: No details accompany this photograph on Exeter incline. However, it is clearly a feast of sound as No 34058 *Sir Frederick Pile* tackles the climb with nine coaches, and with a 'Z' class engine laying into it at the rear. Visible are a Maunsell Corridor Third and 2-set, and several Brake Composites. Down on the right is Exeter West signalbox, at the south end of St David's station. The hills in the background are above Exwick on the far side of the Exe. *Ian Allan Library*

in a deep defile between St Stephens on the right and Launceston itself, distinctive with the squat, lop-sided round tower of its castle, on the skyline to the left. From here it is a very severe 13-mile ascent past the picturesque hamlets of Egloskerry and Splatt, to another bleak, exposed spot called Tinks Corner where a station called Otterham is situated. This station also had its runaway story, when the wagons went down through Launceston and halted away up the other side of the valley at Tower Hill. In a cutting ¾-mile to the west, the line reaches a summit at 860ft. The next 16 miles take it down to sea level.

There is no straight or level track between Egloskerry and Wadebridge Junction, and some of the curves are half-circles. This is partly because, with the notable exceptions of the 86ft-high embankment at Scarsick and a short tunnel under Trelill village, there are few big civil engineering works on the line. It fits into the landscape, rather than slashing a way through it. Through Delabole, which is a no-nonsense working town, and down the Allen valley we are separated from the Atlantic gales by a ridge of high ground, so the country, though hard, is not unpleasant. Approaching the River Camel at Egloshayle it is richly wooded. Incidentally, let us be clear once for all that, the golden camel of Camelford's town hall notwithstanding, the name is a corruption of the Cornish *Carnel* (crooked stream). Wadebridge Junction is not a physical junction, two single lines extending to the station. The other line is of course the Bodmin & Wadebridge of 1834. The only respect in which the 'ACE' could be said to travel on it is that part of Wadebridge station lies on the site of the original terminus.

In this little island most railway tracks are connected with pieces of water of some kind, but for loveliness the Wadebridge to Padstow section is hard to beat. At high tide the water comes up to the lineside, and at low water the acres of sandbanks are an important resort for birds. With continual changes in weather coming in off the ocean, the estuary is never static in shape or mood. Nearing Padstow are two examples of the heroic feats of engineering which are so regrettably undervalued nowadays: the causeway and viaduct over Little Petherick Creek close to the site of one of the very few tide-mills in this country (another Emett inspiration), and a stupendous rock cutting through the shoulder of Dennis Hill. Finally, there is no anticlimax to our long adventure, for here is the sound of seagulls, the smell of fishnets and the sight of the old village and harbour of Padstow.

Table of Maximum Train Loads on Inclines

Exeter St David's–Exeter Central

'M7' class engine	140 tons
'N'	200
'T9'	140
'WC'	200
Max for any train:	*400 tons or 12 bogie coaches.*

Yeoford–Plymouth

Class 2 or 3 engines	230 tons fast,	150 tons stopping
Class 4	270	200
Class 7	350	270

Braunton–Mortehoe

'M7' class engine	140 tons
'N'	180
'T9'	100
'WC'	240
'4500'	150
'6300'	190
LMR Class 2	140

Max for any train: 11 bogie coaches or equivalent

Ilfracombe–Mortehoe

'M7' class engine	140 tons
'N'	180
'T9'	100
'WC'	205
'4500'	140
'6300'	180
LMR Class 2	140

Tipton–Sidmouth

'M7'	160 tons
'O2'	128
BR Class 3 & LMR Class 2	200

Tipton–Exmouth

'M7'	170 tons
'O2'	140
BR Class 3 & LMR Class 2	200

Right: In 1960-62 Plymouth North Road was rebuilt, incorporating a huge new office block to accommodate the increase in managerial posts which always accompanies an economy programme. On 30 April 1962 the Plymouth 'ACE' has deposited its passengers and is moving out empty to the Mount Gould sidings. The engine is No 34110 *66 Squadron,* the last 'West Country' and then only 11 years old. *B. Haresnape*

Right: 'T9' No 30709 brings the Plymouth portion of a London train into North Road from Friary on 24 July 1957. Mutley station lay just round the bend beyond Sutherland Road bridge. *C.P. Boocock*

Right: Having shut off steam, the driver of 'M7' No 30036 leans out to see his signals as he approaches North Road from Mutley Tunnel. His mate has obviously just made up the fire. *R.E. Vincent*

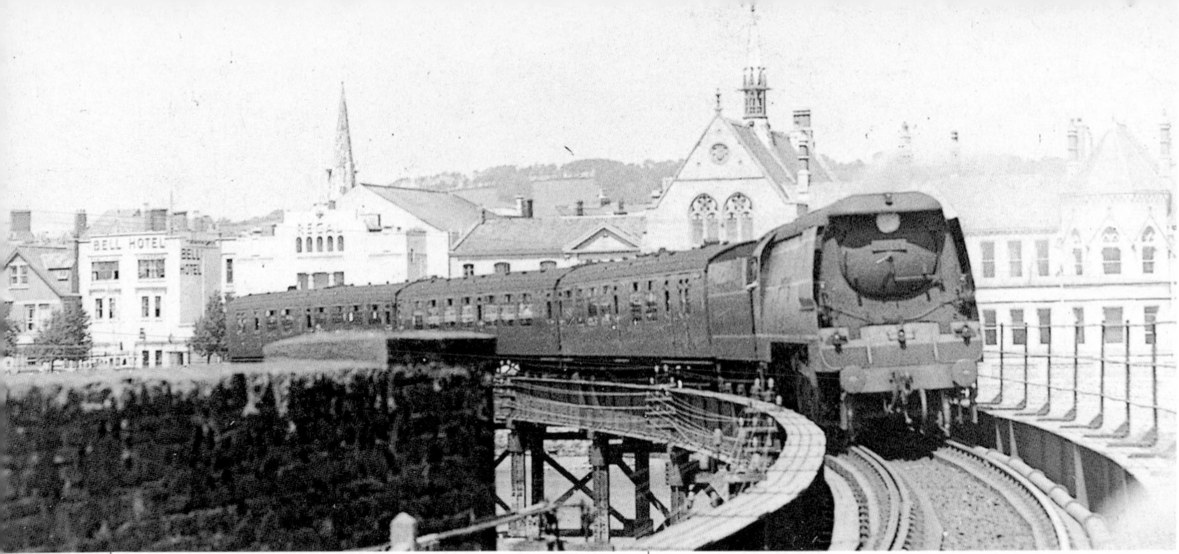

Above: Just north of the following view, but earlier in date, 28 June 1949, the up train rumbles slowly over the Taw bridge. The photographer is not about to be run down; he is looking over the wall from the main road. *M.P. Mileham*

Left: Coming round the curve from the Taw bridge in Barnstaple. The fireman on No 34030 *Watersmeet* is holding the tablet ready to hand to Barnstaple Junction B signalman. There must be a big pipeline project on, as the Sawmilling & General Supplies Co yard is crammed with concrete pipe sections. *J. Davenport*

Left: 'M7' No 30674, built at Nine Elms in 1897 and scrapped in 1961. This shows it shunting coaches at Salisbury station west end; the building behind is the Great Western signalbox. *J. Davenport*

Right: 'T9' No 30338, built at Nine Elms in 1901, reboilered in 1923 and scrapped in 1961. Posed here in the beautiful waterside setting of Padstow turntable on 14 June 1960. *K.R. Pirt*

Locomotives

A look at some of the principal locomotive types associated with the 'ACE'

The 'M7' Class 0-4-4T

Introduced in 1897 for express passenger working, these engines hauled the Exeter–Plymouth trains using the new line from Lydford to Devonport. However, only a year after introduction, No 252 left the road at speed near Tavistock, and consequently engines of this arrangement were deemed unsuitable for such work. They were downgraded to local passenger duties and throughout the 'ACE' era would be seen on the Seaton and Sidmouth branches with the through coach attached to the branch set. In North Devon they served as bankers on the Ilfracombe line, and almost to the end the Torrington portion was an 'M7' duty. Another important job they did was to haul the empty stock between Waterloo and Clapham Yard.

By 1911, 105 had been built and they appeared everywhere, but their long career on the branch lines does not mean that they were well suited to the purpose, as may be seen when they are compared with the '4500' class six-coupled tank engine which the Great Western used for similar work. Although the boiler was about the same size, the grate area was 20½sq ft against 16½, the coupled wheel diameter 5ft 7in against 4ft 7½in, and the weight of 60 tons carried on one less axle than the '4500's 61 tons. Although they could show a good turn of speed on a semi-fast passenger train, their progress was generally steady rather than lively. They were inclined to go up hills at their own pace, like the old grey mare who ignores any impatience shown by the man holding the reins. However, they were solidly built and the motion arrangement was free from the problems of accessibility and high bearing stresses which so often plagued passenger tank engines, so there was no reason why they should not have gone on for ever.

The 'T9' Class 4-4-0 'Greyhounds'

The first of these engines were completed in 1899 and, like many others on the South Western, were built by Dübs & Co of Glasgow. Others were built at Nine Elms, to a total of 66, and none lasted less than 50 years. Although they did not look very big, they had 18½in cylinders and a 24sq ft grate. Their motion layout was similar to that of those other long-lived Drummond classes,

Above: 'N15' No 30785 *Sir Mador de la Porte,* a Glasgow-built engine, seen in final form shortly before withdrawal in 1959. *MNLPS Collection*

Left: An 'S15' on a normal duty, a main line freight heading eastwards down the hill from Buckhorn Weston Tunnel on 2 June 1962. No 30841 was built at Eastleigh in 1936 and sold for scrap in 1964; 10 years later it was restored to working order by a small group, the Essex Locomotive Society, in the goods shed at Chappel station. *G.A. Richardson*

the 'M7' and '700', and they had robust frames and generous bearing surfaces. They were thus able to take the increased power available from superheater boilers, which were fitted from 1922 onwards. In this form they were regarded by many as the best engines the line ever had. They did not run hot bearings, the long wheelbase gave a steady ride, they were light on coal, and when necessary they could be put on a 10-coach Saturday extra with complete confidence.

The famous driver Bert Hooker summed up the 'T9' as an upright engine: the pressure gauge needle was upright, near blowing-off, the regulator handle was upright, half open — and the fireman was upright.

They worked the Padstow and Bude 'ACEs' from Okehampton, and later the Plymouth portion when the priority changed, until the appearance of large numbers of 'West Countries' pushed them down to second-rank duties. In 1937 the 'U1' class express passenger 2-6-0s were tried as replacements but these theoretically much more powerful machines proved inferior in service and were themselves replaced by more 'T9s'. In diminishing numbers they carried on until the very last appearance of the class at Padstow, No 120 on a special train on 27 April 1963.

The 'N15' Class 4-6-0 'King Arthurs'

This, Robert Urie's express engine, combined the solidity of the Drummond tradition with modern valve motion, superheating, accessibility of parts for servicing and attention to construction and repair costs. They had 6ft 7in wheels, 22in cylinders (the largest in Britain) a 30sq ft grate and weighed 78 tons; on paper they were the most

Above: The information on this shot reads: 'Down Atlantic Coast Express, *c*1935, near Surbiton', which leaves quite a lot of choice. The engine is 'LN' No 865 *Sir John Hawkins,* built at Eastleigh in 1929.
Ian Allan Library/LPC

powerful 4-6-0s in the country. When the first ones were delivered from Eastleigh Works in 1918 they were considered very modern, but their performance was well below the standard of their equivalents elsewhere, and Richard Maunsell reworked the design with higher boiler pressure, smaller cylinders, larger steam passages and valve travel, improved draughting and exhaust steam injectors. The first of the new version, No 453 *King Arthur*, was also the first to receive a name. Thirty of the Maunsell 'N15s', Nos 763–792, were built by the North British Locomotive Co and often referred to as 'Scotch Arthurs'. The 20 Urie engines were gradually modified to bring them up to standard with the later ones.

They formed the mainstay of West of England express power until the arrival of Bulleid Pacifics. Even then, the class had its moment of glory when visiting glamour-girl *Mallard* ran hot at Salisbury during the 1948 Trials; No 753 *Melisande* was put on and raced up to Waterloo to regain the lost time. 'N15s' continued to work expresses, including the 'ACE' on occasions, until the 1959 Kent electrification made still more Bulleid Pacifics available. They were free-running and could be worked up to 85mph or more through the dips in order to keep up the overall average. This sort of speed was most unusual in the 1930s and made the Salisbury–Exeter run more exciting than most elsewhere.

We should also include here the similar 'H15' class, with 6ft wheels, and the 'S15', with 5ft 7in wheels, compared with the 6ft 7in of the 'N15'. They were normally booked to semi-fast passenger and freight turns respectively, but could be switched to express work in summer. Even the 'S15s' could be pushed along at 70mph to keep the Saturday timings.

These three classes were approved to work between Cowley Bridge and Okehampton, but they never did so on passenger duties. They were employed on the stone trains from Meldon Quarry, and here again the difference in coupled wheel diameter, so much emphasised by commentators, was less apparent from the point of view of the footplate. Only when extremes of speed or load haulage were called for did it matter whether you had an 'N15' or 'S15'.

The 'LN' Class 4-6-0 'Lord Nelsons'

The 83-ton four-cylinder engine No 850, incorporating the best of current practice, was built at Eastleigh in 1926; 50 similar locomotives were promptly put in hand by the North British Locomotive Co, but they were for the London Midland & Scottish Railway, and two years passed before another 15 were built for the Southern. One was used on Nine Elms Duty No 7, which worked the main 'ACE' to Salisbury and back, but there were not enough of them to cover the summer extras and they never had the chance to make any real contribution to the West of England service. They were not allowed to run west of Exeter.

The 'Nelsons' were very strong engines, but were not quite tuned to long fast runs on a racing ground, so it needed a highly skilled fireman to keep pace with the demand for steam on the Salisbury run. This was shown up when in 1933 they were put to working through between Waterloo and Exeter, and that was soon dropped. Numerous modifications were tried, the most effective being new cylinders with larger valves. However, no more 'LNs' were built

for the West of England line, from which one must conclude that the 'N15s' were considered adequate.

The 'N' Class 2-6-0 'Woolworths'

This class was designed by the South Eastern & Chatham Railway at Ashford in 1914 and was the first application outside the GWR of the taper boiler and long travel valves developed at Swindon. The Southern purchased 50 part-complete engines which had been manufactured at Woolwich Arsenal in a scheme to provide work there during the postwar slump. These entered service in 1924–5. Although their 19in cylinders and 25sq ft grates were comparable with the 'T9s', with bigger boilers and 25% more weight they packed a far bigger punch for lifting heavy loads up the grades west of Exeter and, more importantly, for stopping loads on the way down. They worked the Ilfracombe and Plymouth sections of the 'ACE' until the arrival of the Bulleid Pacifics, and continued to do so occasionally until the end of steam. Besides that, they could do anything, and were the sort of class which is comparatively uninteresting because they were so dependable.

A tank engine version of the larger 'U' class — the Class K 'Rivers' — never worked on the Western Section, but some of them had West

Above: 'N' No 31834, built at Woolwich Arsenal in 1922, at work on 5 August 1950. It is assisting 0-6-0 No 2268 with a Western Region Ilfracombe train, surmounting the bank at Willingcott Bridge. *C.R.L. Coles*

Below right: 'WC' No 34013 *Okehampton,* built in 1945 at Brighton, heading west near Crediton in 1953. Details are not given, but the formation of two 3-sets with a restaurant set between could be the Plymouth portion of the 11.5am down. *R. Russell*

Country names: Nos 804 *River Tamar*, 805 *River Camel*, 806 *River Torridge,* 807 *River Axe*, 808 *River Char* and 809 *River Dart*.

The 'MN' and 'WC' Class 4-6-2 'Merchant Navies' and 'West Countries'

Oliver Bulleid came to the Southern with a firm belief that the Technical Department should lead, not follow, the traffic demands, and his first objective was to provide the power for much faster trains. But on the Southern the provision of more powerful engines was limited by the ability of the road to carry them and the investment in facilities such as turntables. These matters delayed his Pacific until it was overtaken by the war, and the first 'MNs' were

Above: 'MN' No 35023 *Holland-Afrika Line,* only seven months old, at Exeter Central in June 1949. It is standing on the up through road, coupled to the restaurant set, waiting to take over an up 'ACE'. *S.C. Nash*

Right: The same engine after rebuilding in February 1957, in Exmouth Junction shed yard ready to work an 'ACE' on 5 July 1957. 'T9' No 30712 shows the high standard of cleaning typical of this depot and also of Salisbury. *R.C. Riley*

Left: Down 'ACE' approaching Worting Junction in March 1960. It is running on the local line, which beyond the junction becomes the Bournemouth line, so it will have to cross to the adjacent line to continue to Salisbury. The engine, 'MN' No 35028 *Clan Line*, was built at Eastleigh in 1948 and sold for preservation to the Merchant Navy Locomotive Preservation Society in 1967. *MNLPS Collection*

Below: The rebuilt Bulleid Pacific is an impressive machine, and many of the moving parts maintain the South Western tradition of solid construction. The driver of No 35010 *Blue Star* is filling the oil cup on the connecting rod small-end. *MNLPS Collection*

put to work not on ocean liner expresses but on freight.

The first passenger turn worked by a 'Merchant Navy' was in January 1942, between Salisbury and Exeter on the 9am down and 2.30pm up, and they were then put on both parts of the 'ACE'. On 2 December No 21C10 worked a 20-coach test train from Waterloo to Exeter, which resulted in the first scheduled 16-coach 'ACE' run on 4 May 1943, hauled by No 21C9. These massive loads were not plain sailing, as shown when No 21C8 slipped to a standstill on a perfectly dry rail on the 1 in 80 climb from Crewkerne. When an 'MN' was not available two engines, typically an 'N15' and a 'T9', were needed.

There was no doubt about the increase in power; the grate area was two-thirds bigger than that of the 'N15' and the steam you could get from it seemed limitless. The response of the men who had to use them was summed up by the occasion when Bulleid walked up to one, without identifying himself, and genially asked the driver what he thought of it. The driver replied to the effect that, 'It goes very well, but I don't know why the xxxxx has to burn such a lot of coal.' Bulleid gave him a look which would have put the fire out, said, 'Because I designed it to burn a lot of coal,' and retired in good order.

The 'West Country' class arrived with more of a flourish, in peacetime. Many of them, such as *Launceston*, *Bude* and *Tavistock*, had their names unveiled at the stations concerned, with Bulleid and General Manager Sir Eustace Missenden in attendance, promoting much competition among local dignitaries for the privilege, and for the concomitant ride on the engine. They did not do that with *Hartland*, which boasted of being the English parish farthest from a railway station, or with *Yes Tor*, overlooking Okehampton and the

Above: BR Standard Class 4 2-6-4T No 80015, built at Brighton in 1951, drawing into Clapham Yard with an empty train. A Box is surrounded by a steel frame, put up during the war to protect it from incendiaries. An unusual feature of this photograph is that it shows the north side of the train, being taken from the Windsor line station. *MNLPS Collection*

highest point in England south of Kinder Scout. Cornwall's highest peak was not so honoured, presumably on the grounds that respectable patrons would not appreciate travelling behind a *Brown Willy*. The first 'ACE' turn worked was by No 21C101 *Exeter*, from Exeter to Ilfracombe on 11 July 1945.

East of Exeter there was little practical difference between the classes; either was capable of spinning the expresses along the favourable stretches at 80–90mph, something which when performed elsewhere with much lighter trains was held to be marvellous, although the 'WC' with its smaller firebox had less reserve power and gave the fireman more continuous work when being driven hard. West of Exeter, however, there was all the difference, for the 'MNs' were prohibited from running beyond Cowley Bridge Junction. The 'WCs' were lighter, with a coupled axle loading of 18 tons 15cwt instead of the 'MN's 20 tons 17cwt, and this allowed them to run on all the 'ACE' routes except the Lyme Regis branch. 'WCs' which were rebuilt from 1957 had their weight raised by 5½ tons and were then also prohibited west of Cowley Bridge. From 1960 they were allowed to go to Plymouth — and there was at least one occasion when one reached Barnstaple but as always in such cases no one could say how it happened. Consequently the Ilfracombe and Padstow turns remained the

Left: BR Standard Class 3 2-6-2T No 82018, built at Swindon in 1952, at Halwill Junction on 10 April 1956. It has just run round the Maunsell 2-set which constitutes the Bude branch train. *Dr T. Gough*

province of original-condition 'WCs', and one of these, No 34023 *Blackmore Vale*, hauled the very last 'ACE' out of Padstow on 5 September 1964. On that day the 10.35am down was taken to Exeter by rebuilt 'WC'[1] No 34089 *602 Squadron*, and the 11am down by 'MN' No 35022 *Holland-America Line.*

BR 'Standard' Classes

By 1951 trains on the West of England lines, as elsewhere, were being hauled by tank engines up to 70 years old, or by pensioned-off express engines such as the 'S11s' and, while tradition was a fine thing, being able to do the daily oiling without clambering around underneath was a handy improvement. Therefore, so far as budgets permitted, new power was introduced in the form of 'Standard' tank engines, which were well received in spite of being of London Midland & Scottish origin.

The LMS Class 2 2-6-2Ts were used mostly on freight workings and the NDCJR, and their duties on the latter involved them in working the Torrington portion of the 'ACE'. They were also allocated to the Sidmouth and Lyme Regis branches. They were handy little engines, capable of being wound up to quite high power and speed when necessary, unlike the BR Class 2s. Five of those were used by Exmouth Junction from June to September 1961 and sent back east with one comment: 'Useless'.

The authorities felt that something bigger was needed for the duties hitherto performed by the 'M7s'. The Class 3 2-6-2T was reasonably successful on passenger trains and was used on the Bude, Sidmouth and Exmouth branches from 1952 until the end. In their role as 'M7' replacements, some were moved to London in 1962 and took over the empty stock workings. In view of their cost and size — they weighed 74 tons and had a boiler derived from the Swindon 'No 4' as fitted to the '5100s' and '5600s' — they should have performed a great deal better than they did.

Only in the last three years did the Class 4 2-6-4Ts come in, principally on Bude and Ilfracombe duties. These became the most widely used class of steam locomotives in Britain, operating from the South Coast to the north of Scotland. They were big, powerful engines, weighing 87 tons, with a 27sq ft firegrate and 25,000lb nominal tractive effort. Indeed, they were the equal of anything except a 'West Country' and, had the routes west of Exeter survived with steam haulage, they could have handled all the traffic except the long through runs. We might, forsooth, have seen an '80000' tank carrying the 'ACE' headboard through to AD2000 and beyond.

The Diesels

Although the named expresses of the South Western are celebrated as the last in this country to be steam-hauled, they were also the first to be worked regularly by diesel-electric power. Before adopting the Modernisation Plan, the Railway Executive desired proof that the diesels would actually deliver what was promised — specified performance in daily use on a real railway. A large-scale test was mounted on the South Western main lines.

The trials used five locomotives. Nos 10000 and 10001 were built at Derby in 1947 and 1948; the power plant, including a 1,600hp diesel engine, was supplied by English Electric. They ran from Euston to Carlisle and St Pancras to Manchester, then in March 1953 they were moved to Nine Elms. Nos 10201 and 10202 were built at Ashford in 1949–51, also equipped by English Electric, with 1,750hp engines. In March 1954 they were joined by No 10203, built at Brighton and similar except for a 2,000hp engine.

Right: No 10000 passing Durnsford Road generating station with a West of England express. *Ian Allan Library*

Right: No, it doesn't run on water. Filling up the train heating boiler tank on No 10202 after arrival at Exeter Central. This was one of the few moments during an ordinary turn on a diesel when two pairs of hands were actually needed. *W.M.J. Jackson*

These locomotives were put to work on intensive duties which typically entailed two round trips to Exeter daily. The first service run was made by No 10202 on the down 'ACE' on 17 October 1951. They also worked on the Bournemouth route: Duty No 5 in 1954 comprised the 2.45am Waterloo–Bournemouth newspapers and 7.20am return, the down 'ACE' to Exeter and the 4.30pm return. They performed this work quite successfully until March 1955, when they were moved to the London Midland Region at Camden. When No 10203 was completed, the road service diesel locomotive as a concept was only 20 years old, and bearing in mind where the steam locomotive was after 20 years of development, the engineers certainly had nothing to be ashamed of in their achievement.

During 1963 and 1964 the up working from Exeter was diagrammed for a Western Region 'D800' series locomotive. These machines were a very different proposition from the diesel-electrics. The technology of the latter was not new on the Southern, indeed it was older than the Bulleid Pacifics. The diesel engine had been proved in marine service and either it went or it didn't, and the device which actually turned the wheels, an electric motor, had not changed for many years and was thoroughly tried and true. However, D800, built at Swindon in 1958, had two Maybach Type MD650 1,100hp medium-speed engines, each driving a Mekydro hydraulic torque converter with a gear and shaft drive to the wheels. This offered savings in efficiency and weight — the locomotive weighed only 78 tons — over the cumbersome electric generator and motors, but it had two drawbacks. First, it did not have the years of experience behind it which electric traction had on the Southern. Second, the electric motor shares with the steam engine the ability to deliver, for a quarter of an hour or so, a power output far above its continuous rating. In the latter case the energy reserve formed by the water in the boiler diminishes; in the former the equipment gradually gets hotter. The diesel-hydraulic plant lacked this flexibility, which told against it in the punishing conditions of railway service. Time and again a 'Warship' would finish a run on one engine in an aura of hot oil, but for all that, their tribulations were no worse than those of the 'Merchant Navies' or the Drummond 4-6-0s on this line in previous times. Whether they could, in the long run, have handled the volume and variety of traffic that was once shifted by steam is something we may never know.

Visitors

The 10.50am down to Exeter and the 12.42pm up served as the Southern's course for the Exchange Trials in June 1948. The LMSR was represented by No 46236 *City of Bradford* and No 46154 *The Hussar*, and the LNER by No 60022 *Mallard*. The latter ran a hot big end on the first trial and was replaced by No 60033 *Seagull*. The GWR did not contend; their engines were too big for the Southern loading gauge. The home team fielded No 35018 *British India Line*. The trials were unusual in that the engines were worked by crews from their home railways, rather than local men. (In steam days, the men were expected to do the job with whatever type of engine was provided, regardless of whether they were familiar with it or had even seen one before.) Ironically, the best running was achieved by the smallest engine, No 46154.

The trials attracted a great deal of public interest, but they provided no information on such important subjects as reliability, load haulage potential, acceleration or braking performance, so in retrospect they look like little more than a piece of fun for the managers; and the only definite result was to confirm the accountants in their belief that one steam locomotive is much like another.

During May 1953, while the 'Merchant Navies' were out of action following the Crewkerne accident when No 35020 broke her crank axle, the other regions helped out, and 'Britannias' and 'V2s' appeared on the West of England trains. Photographer Ivo Peters noted the 10.54 and 11.0 down 'ACEs' on 23 May hauled by Nos 60928 and 70029 *Shooting Star* respectively.

The Man on the Shovel

No one would have gone to the Atlantic coast at all were it not for the labours of the men who shovelled coal into tenders and fireboxes, and shovelled ash and clinker out of fireboxes, smokeboxes and pits. At the start of our period the typical West of England express was hauled by an engine weighing some 50 tons, with a grate area of 25sq ft. At the end the engine weighed 93 tons and the firegrate was 50sq ft. However, the man who fired it was not enlarged or redesigned in any way. This vast increase in the size of the job seems to have been taken for granted by every commentator. It is only proper that any review of motive power should conclude with a tribute to the men who made it go.

[1] *Purists will say that No 34089 was a member of the 'Battle of Britain' class; however, this sub-class of the 'WCs' was technically identical, the different class name being given for publicity purposes to those engines named in commemoration of the Battle and originally allocated to the Southeast.*

Left & Below left: Two pictures of the up 'ACE' during the trials, ascending the 1 in 100 incline out of Black Boy Road Tunnel and past Exmouth Junction marshalling yard. The archaic-looking coach conceals what was then highly sophisticated equipment, including automatic gas analysers and mechanical computers for monitoring engine performance. Its principal apparatus was a calibrated drawbar spring, linked to a distance-measuring wheel to determine the power output, this device being called a dynamometer. These are the two LMSR entrants, No 46154 *The Hussar* and No 46236 *City Of Bradford*.
B. Marshall/E.W.J. Crawforth

5

Coaches

The coach which characterised the 'ACE' was the Brake Composite; containing First and Third class seating, a lavatory and a luggage compartment, it was a complete train in itself and formed one of the divided portions when only one coach was needed. The larger portions (Ilfracombe having three coaches all the year round) were usually formed from three-coach sets, and if necessary further single coaches from the 'loose' stock, not formed into sets, were added. The restaurant service was provided by a kitchen/dining coach, or latterly a kitchen/buffet coach, paired with a dining saloon.

Prewar

The premier vehicles available in 1926 were the LSWR design of 1921; 57ft long, with elliptical roofs and the most modern interior fittings. Built to the maximum permitted width, they were distinguished by having the luggage area sides set in to leave room to provide the guard's compartment with a small forward lookout. They were known as 'Ironclads' because although the body frame and roof were of wood, the sides were made of sheet steel.

Although these coaches were soon replaced on the top-rank services, they continued in use on the local and branch line trains which had the 'ACE' portions attached to them. The Seaton branch train was a pair of 'Ironclads' until the end of 1962, and sets of them were available for summer extras until 1959. Some outlived the 'ACE' itself, as mess and tool vans for engineering and breakdown trains.

The Southern settled on an improved version of the LSWR design, with 59ft bodies, a new type of bogie with wheelbase reduced from 9ft to 8ft, and detail changes such as Buckeye automatic couplings and Pullman-type gangway connectors. The construction was the same. Coupling the new stock to the 'Ironclads' was inconvenient, as the latter had the old standard gangways and screw couplings. New three-car sets were available for July 1926, but Brake Composites did not come along until August. The three-car sets comprised a Composite and two Brake Thirds, nearly half of whose length was given over to luggage space, for the travellers of those days were mostly middle-class and took masses of luggage, knowing that every station had porters awaiting them. The set seated 24 First and 88 Third. There were 10 Brake Composites, all were allocated to the 'ACE' and on paper all were running every day. Each seated 12 First and 32 Third, had one lavatory and a fairly small luggage area. A normal winter train made up with these would seat 120 First and 344 Third.

LSWR dining cars were used until July 1930, when new kitchen/dining cars were built. Each had 12 First seats and was paired with a dining car termed 'Nondescript', which could be configured for First, Second or Third class[1] according to demand and seated 42 diners. By then another 50 Brake Composites were in service, and all the West of England trains were made up of new coaches.

Two complete sets were required to operate each daily service. In general, the trains reached their western destinations too late to take up any return working to London, so they had to stay there overnight, and only made one round trip in two days. On arrival at Waterloo the portions would be in the wrong order for a westbound working, so they were remarshalled at Clapham Yard during the night, as well as being cleaned. The Southern's aim was for all coaches to be swept out and windows cleaned daily, and externally washed every three days. Anyone who is inclined to take coach cleaning for granted is recommended to try it, working from ground level with buckets and brooms, preferably in winter. This work, as well as virtually all other rolling stock servicing, was carried out in the open in all weathers. It was obviously vastly improved by the provision at Clapham Junction of a servicing shed in 1927 and a mechanical cleaning plant in 1934. The latter, for those who have not seen it, was the precursor of the modern car wash and worked in the same way; trains were drawn slowly through it on their way into the depot.

The restaurant sets, when working only as far as Exeter on the 11am down, returned on the

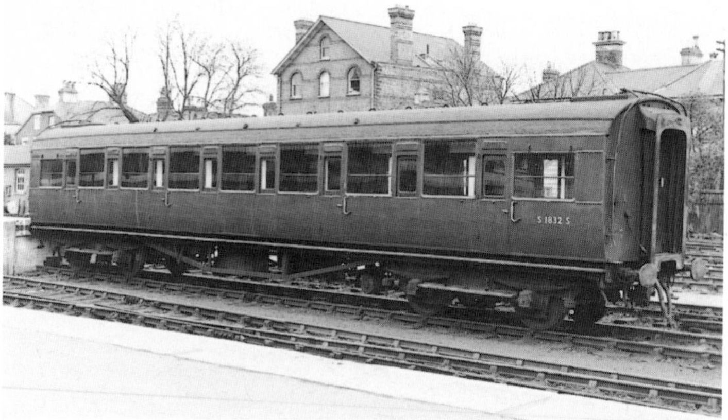

Above: Set No 250 is a typical Maunsell 3-set. This shows it as it was between 1951 and 1961, comprising Brake Thirds Nos 2785 and 2786 and Composite No 5655. It is in a famous location, half-way up Honiton bank, on 3 August 1955, being hauled by a notable engine. 'S15' No 30847 was the last Southern 4-6-0, in December 1936. Sold in 1964, it lay in a scrapyard for 20 years until going to the Bluebell Railway, where a rebuild was completed in 1994. *J. Robertson*

Above left: Corridor Third No 1832, built at Eastleigh in 1934, was in service for just 30 years. *T.C. Robbins*

Left: On 6 July 1957, the first four vehicles of the 8.10am Torrington/8.10 Ilfracombe/8.15 Plymouth, as it leaves Exeter, are Maunsell stock; 2-set No 24, a dining car and kitchen/buffet, the latter still in red and cream livery. The four cattle vans by the pens remind us that in those days the transport of livestock was done by train, in strictly controlled conditions. *R.C. Riley*

Right: Bulleid coaches on through workings sometimes found themselves joined to very old vehicles indeed, like this prewar (first, that is) set. The 9.50am to Sidmouth Junction leaving Exmouth on 17 June 1949; engine No 669. *S.C. Nash*

4.30pm to Waterloo. In the summer, when restaurant sets ran through to Ilfracombe and Bude, and later to Torrington and Padstow, they also stayed overnight, and so perforce did their crews. Old coaches (usually 'Ironclads') fitted out as dormitories were placed at those stations for their use. (They were similar to the provision made for enginemen, but of course segregation was absolute.)

Through the 1930s, two eight-car trains, including dining sets, were used on summer Saturdays for the 10.35am down to Ilfracombe and the 10.30am up, and spent the rest of the week in Wimbledon Park sidings. Indeed, there were 18 complete trains which went out only on summer Saturdays, for the total West of England service needed 32 sets then, but only 14 on summer weekdays and 10 for the rest of the year.

In the postwar years the coaches were gradually downgraded in favour of new stock. In 1948, and again in 1958, some were re-formed into two-car sets which provided the local services west of Exeter and on the East Devon branches. In this capacity they were found heading for Bude, Sidmouth, etc, with the through coach, distinguished by its different shape and destination boards, coupled on at the rear. The kitchen/dining cars, unused as such in the later years of the war, were rebuilt as buffet cars and used on the less important expresses.

Others finished up as another small part of the service; camping coaches. They were offered at Combpyne, Tipton St John's, Newton Poppleford, East Budleigh, Littleham, Wrafton, Whitstone, Bere Ferrers and Port Isaac Road. The latter was, and is, an exposed spot miles from anywhere and was soon taken off the list.

Postwar

O.V.S. Bulleid took an interest in coach design and, with Sir Herbert Walker elevated to the board, he and General Manager A.W. Szlumper set about creating a new image. The side profile was a sleek curve, length was increased to 64ft, compartment doors were replaced by picture windows, the interior was brightened with light veneers, chrome plating and mirrors. The bodies were painted in a light green which reputedly was chosen arbitrarily by Walker, from a piece of yarn he bought in a haberdashery on the spur of the moment. The construction was not very far advanced from the LSWR design. Steel floor plates between the doors and some ribs of steel channel were welded to the frame, but the rest of the framing was wood with a wooden canvas-covered roof and steel side cladding. Apart from the welded attachments, it was theoretically possible to strip the coach down to the underframe with a screwdriver.

The prototype of the new coach design was completed in September 1945 but meanwhile some three-car sets halfway between the new and the old were built, and appeared on the Plymouth and Ilfracombe 'ACEs' for a couple of years. The first production set to the new design was put on the 'ACE' at the end of 1946. In it most of the Third class seats were in open saloons; hitherto passengers had preferred compartments but the new generation of working-class holidaymakers were presumed to be more gregarious, and of course the saloon layout was cheaper. Over the next three years two- and three-car sets and Brake Composites were built in quantity and served until the end.

Each three-car set comprised two Brake Thirds and a Composite. It seated 24 First and 120 Third. The Brake Third was divided into three: the guard and luggage, two compartments and a lavatory, and an open saloon. This layout was referred to as 'semi-open'. The last of these sets were completed in June 1950, and were thereafter normally increased to five cars for the

Left: Still in full Southern livery, as it is 13 March 1948 and they have only just been taken over by the Government, Bulleid Semi-open Brake Third No 4335 behind engine No 21C7 *Aberdeen Commonwealth. British Railways/MNLPS Collection*

summer by the addition of two Corridor Thirds.

The two-car set comprised a semi-open Brake Third and a Brake Composite. The latter had guard and luggage, two First compartments, four Third compartments and a lavatory. The set seated 12 First and 80 Third.

The single Brake Composite had guard and luggage, two First compartments, a lavatory and four Third compartments, seating 12 First and 32 Third. A typical winter train made up of Bulleid stock would seat 108 First and 344 Third, so it was similar to the prewar accommodation; however, the summer strengthening coaches were likely to be Open Thirds or Corridor Thirds, seating 64, which reflected the decline in First Class clientele.

In these coaches the construction of the seats was relatively simple: basically a metal rack with a cushion, surrounded by hardboard panels trimmed with leathercloth and moquette. However, the proportions, padding and springing were so exactly right that the seats were marvellously comfortable. The writer's experience during preservation work was that it was unwise to sit down on one of the completed seats for a tea-break, as one was most reluctant to get up again. Long journeys down to Cornwall were no hardship on the sitter's sit-upon.

During the 1950s BR Standard coaches began to appear; although these were very different in construction, with all-steel, all-welded bodies, their passenger accommodation was virtually identical to the Bulleid coaches, so from the traffic point of view they could be treated as interchangeable. During the last couple of years an 'ACE' was quite likely to be formed partly or wholly of 'Standards'. The most conspicuous feature to distinguish them from Bulleid coaches in photographs is the absence of a little oval window in the top of the door.

There were also some non-passenger vehicles involved. Except during the summer, the up Torrington coach was accompanied as far as Exeter by one or two bogie vans. These were from the 1.10am down newspaper train, being returned empty to London. The four-wheeled parcels vans, which the Southern was so fond of adding to its trains, were sometimes included but not east of Exeter, as they would have brought the train over the load limit.

In the postwar era some attempt was made to increase the use of the coaches. For example, the set arriving at Ilfracombe was used for the 8.30pm to Barnstaple on the same evening, returning at 8.0 the next morning, and the Plymouth set formed the 9.15pm to Tavistock and 6am return. Utilisation was still generally low. When a restaurant set was provided from Ilfracombe or Padstow on a Saturday up service, it was hauled down with the kitchen car as dead weight, unmanned, on the Friday train, and the down set was returned in the same way on Sunday.

The coaches which attracted the most attention, indeed notoriety, were the Tavern Cars. These were the first to include a buffet counter adjoining the kitchen, and incorporated two other important features: attractive looking but not too comfortable wooden seats in the buffet area, and accompanying dining cars with no windows except for small drawlights near the roof. This was intended to speed up the flow of customers, since they could not see out while dining and would not be tempted to linger. The dining car seated 24 First and 40 Third; the Tavern had no dining seats, just 12 seats in the buffet area. The buffet interior was decorated with oak seating and beams, imitation rough plastered walls and ceiling, metal lanterns, leaded windows and tile pattern floor. However, the functional parts of the vehicle used modern equipment and materials. On the outside, the famous Tavern look was obtained by a white pattern on the red paint and black lines on the cream upper part. The inn signs were painted by Joan Main and David Cobb, and the oak used for the interior beams was claimed to have been at Eastleigh Works for 12 years.

The concept was very successful, the Taverns having the best takings of any catering vehicles on the railways. The Hotels Executive, which on Nationalisation took over the catering operations of the railway companies, had realised that train catering was becoming unprofitable. For the year 1950 it only just covered its labour and supplies costs, and if the cost of the coaches and the fuel used in hauling them about was added, the result was a loss of £600,000. Massive price increases or wholesale withdrawals of the services were not realistic options, so amelioration was tried with the introduction of the buffets and, in March 1951, price rises which were hefty enough: luncheon, 5s to 6s[2]; afternoon tea 1s 6d to 2s; dinner 5s to 6s; and breakfast 4s to 4s 6d.

The Taverns were launched on 25 May 1949 under the slogan: 'There is a tavern on the train'. No doubt the décor took most observers by surprise, for it looked funny, and in postwar England no one was supposed to have fun. Once the Press noticed them, humorists had a field day. They helped inspire Emett's fantastical railway in the Festival of Britain funfair beside the line in Battersea, but Lancaster of the *Daily Express* called them 'the height of absurdity'. The first

Right: First-series Brake Composite No 6709, built in 1948 and scrapped at the end of 1967. There were only 13 coaches of this type, formed in 2-coach sets and used exclusively on West of England services. *T.C. Robbins*

Right: Corridor Third No 94, built in 1950 and scrapped in 1967, has been shunted into the cattle pens siding at Exeter Central after providing accommodation for Exeter passengers on an up train. *T.C. Robbins*

service run was on the 10.35am down on Saturday 28 May; two sets were allocated to the 'ACE', but the other six went to the Eastern Region.

The furore which brought the Taverns to the front pages of the newspapers was mixed up with a quite different protest, headed by the Methodist Church and the National United Temperance League, against the serving of alcohol on trains. That had first been voiced in 1946 and flared up on the arrival of coaches that imitated pubs. A vitriolic campaign against the Taverns themselves was led by a Sheffield model railway enthusiast, and under threat of a boycott by some influential patrons, the sets were brought back to the Southern during the autumn. From July 1950 the dining cars were rebuilt with conventional seating and windows, and from 1959 the Taverns were refitted in contemporary buffet style.

The drinks tariff at that time was: tea 3d, coffee 4d, sherry 2s 6d, whisky 2s 3d, draught bitter 1s 10d a pint.

Fares

The price of a ticket is a subject of great importance to anyone travelling on or operating a railway. What seems amazing to those of us of the postwar generation, used to continuous rapid inflation, is that from 1926 until the outbreak of war the fares hardly rose at all, as is shown in these examples:

Specimen Fares From London

Ordinary Return

	1926		1937		1947		1962	
	1st	*3rd*	*1st*	*3rd*	*1st*	*3rd*	*1st*	*2nd*
Ilfracombe	84s 2d	50s 6d	84s 2d	50s 6d	117s 10d	70s 8d	141s	94s
Torrington	84s 2d	50s 6d	84s 8d	50s 10d	118s 6d	71s 2d	141s	94s
Plymouth	93s 4d	56s	93s 10d	56s 4d	131s 4d	78s 10d	153s	102s
Padstow	106s 8d	64s	106s 6d	64s	149s 2d	88s 6d	165s	110s
Bude	95s 4d	57s 2d	95s 4d	57s 2d	133s 6d	80s	156s	104s
Sidmouth	70s	42s	70s	42s	98s	58s 10d	115s 6d	77s
Exmouth	73s 4d	44s	73s 4d	44s	102s 8d	61s 6d	121s 6d	81s

Left: 3-set No 819, comprising Brake Thirds Nos 4277 & 4278 with Composite No 5812 between them, was built by the Birmingham Railway Carriage & Wagon Co in 1948. It is seen behind No 34058 *Sir Frederick Pile*, entering Bere Alston station on 9 September 1962. The Callington branch doubles back beyond the first field on the right. *L. Nicholson*

Above: BR Standard Brake Second No S34621 shows the generous luggage area provided on these vehicles. The location is again Exeter Central, looking east past A Box, on 1 September 1962. The engine is No 34081 *92 Squadron*, another one which survived the scrapyard to be preserved. *Ian Allan Library*

The habit of quoting fares in shillings was a quaint little piece of snobbery on the part of the railway managers, who regarded the pound sterling as slightly vulgar. They liked to see themselves as part of the class of society that bought its clothes in guineas.

Third Class was designated Second from June 1956.

In 1926 the Ordinary Return was valid for two months. There was also a Tourist Return at a reduced fare which operated during May to October (the idea of a railway actually encouraging holiday travel sounds unreal at the end of the century). Much cheaper were Weekend Returns, valid for the outward journey after midday Friday and all day Saturday, and Period Excursions, Third Class only, available on certain specified Friday trains with return eight or 15 days later.

Examples of these, again from London, are:

W'loo to	**Ord Return**		**Tourist Return**		**Weekend Return**	
	1st	*3rd*	*1st*	*3rd*	*1st*	*3rd*
Barnstaple	78s 4d	47s	72s	43s 3d	52s 3d	31s 6d
Bideford	82s 2d	49s 4d	75s 6d	45s 3d	55s	33s
Bude	95s 4d	57s 2d	87s 6d	52s 6d	63s 9d	38s 3d
Budleigh Salterton	71s 4d	42s 10d	65s 6d	39s 6d	47s 9d	28s 9d
Exeter	71s 8d	43s	65s 9d	39s 6d	48s	28s 9d
Exmouth	73s 4d	44s	67s 3d	40s 6d	49s	29s 6d
Ilfracombe	84s 2d	50s 6d	77s 3d	46s 6d	56s 3d	33s 9d
Launceston	91s 4d	54s 10d	83s 9d	50s 6d	61s	36s 9d
Okehampton	82s 6d	49s 6d	75s 9d	45s 6d	55s	33s
Padstow	106s 8d	64s	98s	58s 9d	71s 3d	42s 9d
Plymouth	93s 4d	56s	85s 9d	51s 6d	62s 3d	37s 6d
Sidmouth	70s	42s	64s 3d	38s 6d	46s 9d	28s
Tavistock	88s 10d	53s 4d	81s 6d	49s	59s 3d	35s 9d
Torrington	84s 2d	50s 6d	77s 3d	46s 6d	56s 3d	33s 9d

Children under 12 went half-fare, children under three went free if accompanied by a full-fare payer. The free luggage allowance was 150lb for First Class and 100lb for Third Class. Tickets were issued for dogs, bicycles and perambulators.

The complicated variations in fares came in for a lot of criticism, and were greatly simplified over the next decade. In 1947, the Southern Railway's last operating year, there was a Monthly Return at just over two-thirds the Ordinary Return, available on any train. The age limit for half-fare children was raised to 14. By 1962 the ticket structure had once more degenerated into a farrago of Circular Tours, Cheap Day Returns, Excursions, Mid-Week Period Reduced Fares, Holiday Runabouts, Short Period Seasons and Rail-Rovers. Bearing in mind that the train might also have on board parties booked at various rates according to their numbers and ages, ticket inspection called for quick thinking and a capacious memory.

[1] The Southern retained Second class for the Boat Train traffic.

[2] A reminder of pre-decimal currency; there were 20 shillings (s) to the pound and 12 pence (d) to the shilling. 1s = 5p; the luncheon and dinner price increase equates to a rise from 25p to 30p!

Below: The Southern Region made up its BR Standard coaches into sets in the manner of their predecessors, and this is a 3-set forming the 11.50am Plymouth-Exeter on 29 April 1962; engine No 34070 *Manston*. It is running off Shillamill Viaduct south of Tavistock, one of the loveliest of all West Country viaducts. *J.C. Beckett*

Above right: A Composite Restaurant Car, or 'Tavern Trailer'. The number is not visible, but it could be No 7840, which ran with No 7898 for many years on 'The Royal Wessex'. These two photographs were taken on the Weymouth Harbour branch. *T.C. Robbins*

Right: A Tavern Car, in its later configuration with a pair of ordinary windows at the far (buffet area) end. The windows at the near end are the crew mess compartment and lavatory. This is No 7898, formerly named *The Green Man. T.C. Robbins*

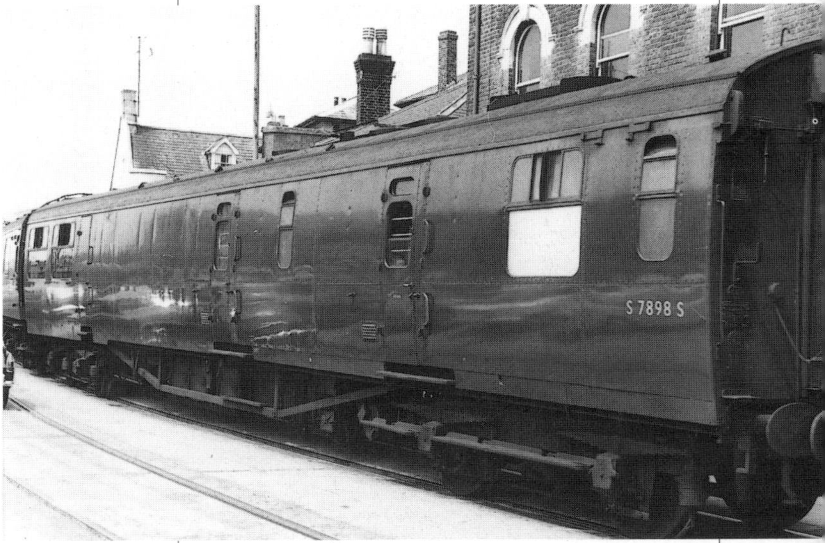

Right: The more numerous type of Brake Composite, which ran loose and formed the one-coach portions of trains such as the 'ACE'. This is No 6729, built in 1948 and kept in service until the end of 1967, seen near the end of that period at Bournemouth Central. *T.C. Robbins*

Above: The Slade valley, above Ilfracombe. The down 'ACE' on 13 September 1963 uses a BR Standard set. *J. Scrace*

Left: On board a train climbing the Slade valley, nearing the tunnel. It is the 2.12pm through train to Waterloo, conveying the empty newspaper van; engine No 34011 *Tavistock. K.A. Stone/E.W.J. Crawforth Collection*

Below: On 4 July 1964, the passengers leaving a train at Ilfracombe show the sort of patrons left to the railway: all are adults, the men wearing suits and ties in midsummer. No 34023 *Blackmore Vale,* the first 'West Country' to be preserved, runs round. *K.A. Stone/E.W.J. Crawforth Collection*

6

The Resorts

Ilfracombe

One of the few places on the north Devon coast to have a good natural harbour, it has been a port since ancient times. It faces across the Bristol Channel to the Gower in South Wales, which is clearly visible from the high ground behind the town. The dramatic cliff scenery made the area popular with tourists — the well-off of course — who arrived by sea before the railways were built, and a shortage of accessible sandy beaches was met with typical Victorian energy by boring pedestrian tunnels through the cliffs. There was just room for a garden, bandstand and theatre. The population was 9,200 in 1957.

The railway suffered, here as in many picturesque places, from being unable to reach the town. The descent from Willingcott at 1 in 36 is the second steepest on a main-line railway in the country, but the station perched high over the town on a promontory called The Cairn. The steep streets up to it were rapidly built up with hotels and elegant town houses. The two-platform station was enlarged in 1928 and provided with seven carriage sidings and a 65ft turntable for the 'N' class engines, replaced in 1950 by a 70ft one for the 'West Countries'.

The run to and from Barnstaple was a slow one, as lengthy stops were made at Braunton and Mortehoe for passengers bound for the extensive sands of Saunton and Woolacombe. Banking engines were needed on that 1 in 36, and on the 1 in 40 climb of the other side of the hill from Braunton, and were detached at Mortehoe. They were permitted to be coupled on the front of trains weighing less than 280 tons, but had to be on the rear of those heavier than that. The full-length summer through trains usually needed both. To ensure that what went up came down safely, all trains over 180 tons had two brake vans. Understandably, vehicles were never left at the Ilfracombe end of Mortehoe station during shunting!

The Great Western also ran its own trains through between Taunton and Ilfracombe, detaching or attaching Ilfracombe portions at Barnstaple South Junction. Locomotives were almost invariably '6300' series 2-6-0s.

Torrington

Here the station was over 200ft below the town and a mile from it, on a cramped level space beside the River Torridge. Torrington is a hilltop market town in the heart of a quiet farming district. The little station was mainly a convenient place to park the trains after unloading at Bideford, a port and resort with a 1957 population of 10,100 against Torrington's 2,800. Bideford's station is in East-the-Water, the town proper lying across the Torridge and presenting a charming riverside promenade. Behind the hill at the back of the town lies the district's only purpose-built seaside resort, whose name of Westward Ho! is the title of a novel written by Charles Kingsley in the Royal Hotel at Bideford. The popular commentator S.P.B. Mais enraged the populace by calling it 'moribund', but he probably saw it out of season.

Bude

In the publicity, the northwest Cornish beaches are eulogised as 'great for surfing', which means that for much of the time they are cold and windswept. For miles the blue Atlantic breaks onto sharp rocks at the feet of the cliffs of this beautiful but dangerous coastline — the writer can vouch for its wildness, having stood on the summit of Rough Tor on even a moderately brisk day and watched the spray lashing Varley Head over nine miles away.

Bude shelters at the mouth of the River Neet and was the seaport for the much larger town of Stratton. It gradually became a resort in its own right, although by 1957 its resident population had reached no more than 5,200. The lack of development is largely due to the late arrival of the railway, which was not extended from Holsworthy until 1898. From the station a branch ran down to the basin of the Bude Canal, which is a unique engineering work. In one respect it was the most advanced transport system this country has ever seen, for it was the only one designed to be used by amphibious vehicles. Instead of using locks, its boats ran on rails on water-powered inclined planes — a combination of water and

rail, the two most efficient methods known for moving loads. Ironically, its closure was hastened by the completion of the railway.

Padstow

This is the writer's favourite; even at the end of the 20th century, surrounded by gimcrack bungalows, awash with cars and tourists, the little town still has a Cornish heart. Offering shelter from the ocean gales, it is still a lively port, although difficult to enter because of the obstruction of the Doom Bar, a sandbank thrown up by a mermaid in revenge against a fisherman who interfered with her.

Despite the massive contemporary development of the Metropole Hotel, the town, of only 2,800 inhabitants during the railway era, never grew to resemble the Great Western's Cornish resorts only a few miles away. The station was built on an artificial platform, which was extended as late as 1947 to make room for a 70ft turntable. The fish shed, tidal basin and outer quay were built by the LSWR in 1910. It was the only place in the west where the 'ACE' passenger could alight beside water and straightway see the open sea, an appropriate finale for the longest run in the train's repertoire.

Coasters could come up on the tide to Wadebridge, which like Padstow can trace its history to the fifth century. It was to improve transport inland from there that Sir William Molesworth, the principal landowner, founded the Bodmin & Wadebridge Railway in 1831. This line terminated in the town centre on quays on both sides of the 15th-century bridge, which carried what became the main motor road down the coast. In later years this charming town was chiefly celebrated for traffic jams.

Plymouth

Having read in the history books about the seafarers who set out from here, the mother of 40 Plymouths all over the world, stand on the Hoe looking over the vast sweep of Plymouth Sound

Above: Bude; a view from the end of the track on 1 July 1964. On the left is the station, with a local train just arrived behind 2-6-4T No 80035; on the right the stock of a through train is berthed in the carriage siding. *K.A. Stone/ E.W.J. Crawforth Collection*

Left: Torrington was not a terminus. LMS 2-6-2Ts Nos 41216 and 41283 are heading into the pastoral peace of the North Devon & Cornwall Junction Railway, which begins with a long viaduct over the River Torridge immediately south of the station. The other bridge is the main road to Bideford. *J.C. Beckett*

Above: Torrington station might have been designed as a basis for a model railway: a neat stone-built house and goods shed, an engine shed beyond the house on the left, the grass bank along the back with a group of typical railway staff houses. The town of Great Torrington is on the level of the hill-top. This view was taken on 3 October 1965, and the train is the Southern Counties Touring Society's 'Exeter Flyer'. *R. Fisher*

and feel her achievement, then turn to the massive war memorial and feel the price she has paid. This is a large commercial conurbation, but the proximity of the sea improves the atmosphere, figuratively and literally. The reconstruction of the bombed shopping centre, with broad car-free streets, formed a telling contrast with the general mess that prevailed at the same period at the other end of the line in London.

With a quarter of a million residents, the city alone has half as many people as the whole of Cornwall, but the Southern's presence had a branch-line air. The South Western route down into the Tamar valley, opened on 2 June 1890, was an impressive and expensive piece of engineering, with the Tavy Bridge, Tamerton Viaduct, Ford Viaduct and the Ford and Devonport Park Tunnels to bring it into what had been the terminus at Devonport King's Road. Friary station was built on the site of the Carmelite friary, built in 1314, near Sutton Pool, the original port. North Road station lies in Pennycomequick, Celtic for 'At the head of the creek'. Ford was named after a ford across Keyham Creek; Keyham and Camel's Head both come from the ancient name Kemel. St Budeaux is named after Bishop Budoc, who built a church by Tamerton Creek in AD480.

In 1958 Friary passenger station was closed and the site used to extend the goods station. The only effect this had on the trains was that they left North Road empty and ran into some new carriage sidings off Mount Gould Junction, but the public timetable gave the impression that the Plymouth times had suddenly become 11min faster.

Exmouth

An ancient port, the seaside resort of Exeter's merchants, and close enough for them to live there and travel in daily, to such an extent that it developed a commuter business which was unique in the West Country. The long sandy beach and 2-mile promenade look both out to sea and across the River Exe towards Dawlish Warren. It was

Left: The 2pm Bodmin North-Padstow, No 30712 with 2-set No 66, about a mile west of Wadebridge where the estuary broadens out, on 19 August 1958. *C. Hogg*

Below: No 34110 *66 Squadron* passing Oldtown Cove on the run down to Padstow, on 1 July 1961. *Dr T. Gough*

Above right: Padstow; this end of the town dominated by the bulk of the Hotel Metropole. No 34080 *74 Squadron*, smoking well and blowing-off, is moving off with the 'ACE' at 9.33am on 7 July 1964. The newspaper train from London, which arrived at 9.22, appears to be still standing at the far end of the platform. *K.A. Stone/ E.W.J. Crawforth Collection*

Right: This view over the approaches to Plymouth Friary on 2 September 1958 contains various period items: advertisement posters for Esso, Guinness, Firestone and Players; a lorry labelled 'Gas Service' parked in Knighton Road; 68-year-old 'O2' No 30183 shunting much younger brake-fitted vans; a 25-ton bogie brake van; a Bulleid Brake Composite; an LSWR 'Gate' 2-set used on the Callington branch; a BR Standard Brake Second and a PMV van.
L.W. Rowe

Below: No 34034 *Honiton* passing Plymouth Friary locomotive depot on 15 April 1956. The station is beyond the bridge in the distance. There are three running lines, the nearer one being the Turnchapel branch.
Dr T. Gough

Above: The Exe Estuary is in the background of this view of the 11.50am to Sidmouth Junction setting out across the arches from Exmouth on 17 June 1949. The engine is 'O2' No 224.
S.C. Nash/E.W.J. Crawforth Collection

Below: A train from Tipton running in to Exmouth station on 16 August 1959.
K.A. Stone/E.W.J. Crawforth Collection

the nearest thing which the Southern possessed in these parts to the big resorts developed by the Great Western, but it could only be reached from London by reversing and trundling down a branch line. The link from Budleigh Salterton (a more exclusive watering-place) was built in 1903 to meet with the direct line from Exeter, when the station was replaced by one as big as Plymouth Friary. Exmouth grew rapidly; the population was 17,200 in 1957 and was close on 30,000 30 years later, and it is the only 'ACE' terminus to retain a train service up to the time of writing.

Sidmouth
It could be said to have started the West Country holiday boom, for the Duke and Duchess of Kent and the young Princess Victoria stayed here in 1819, and where Royalty led the descending echelons of society would follow. Sidmouth was unique among 'ACE' stations in having a railway-owned hotel — the Knowle — just down the road from the station. It had 65 bedrooms and central heating, and charged 10 guineas a week. It was built in 1809 as a country house and was a hotel by 1904. Requisitioned by the Royal Air Force during the war, it was bought by the Southern Railway on 4 October 1947, but only two years later the Hotels Executive declared it (and the Manor House Hotel at Moretonhampstead) unremunerative. It was sold to a local solicitor in 1951, and later became the headquarters of the East Devon District Council.

The station had the common drawback of a long uphill walk from the sea front. It was the archetypal branch terminus, with a substantial house, one island platform, a goods shed, loading ramp and coal siding, and a tiny engine shed with a turntable. It was quite inappropriate for a town of 10,400 inhabitants, but the latter's reputation for being exclusive and scorning tourists, effectively discouraged improvement.

Seaton
The port of Axmouth was busy long before the Romans came, but after it became silted up, it was moribund until this resort grew by the long shingle beach. The town is built entirely for the purposes of holiday and retirement, though is not necessarily the worse for that. The branch line much resembled the Sidmouth branch, but instead of winding down a wooded valley it crossed a wide-open estuary to terminate on the foreshore — a bleak setting in winter. The establishment of Warner's holiday camp nearby promised a major expansion. Seaton Junction was improved and enlarged in 1928, and Seaton station was rebuilt in art deco concrete in 1936, but with two platforms and no siding space it was still inadequate. The expansion of the town from its 1950s population of 3,000 took place after the line closed.

The concrete bridge over the mouth of the River Axe is of interest, as it was built by the railway company in 1877.

Lyme Regis
With its beach, harbour and prospects of the cliffs along to Golden Cap, the highest sea cliff in England, this was a fashionable resort long before the railway era. On the huge curve of coastline from Portland Bill to Start Point, it is at the innermost point and is sheltered from all but the fiercest weather. The harbour dates from around 1284, when the title 'Regis' was bestowed by King Edward I, and lies at the foot of a steep main street which remained picturesque until the advent of mass motoring. The station lay as near to the town as it could get, which was still too far away, on a ledge above the River Lim.

The line was of the sort which delights railway enthusiasts but leaves ordinary people totally unimpressed; it took 6¾ tortuous miles to link two points 4⅓ miles apart. It was built as cheaply as possible, even the lofty Cannington Viaduct presenting an aspect of lightness approaching fragility, resulting in expense and inconvenience in operating throughout its life. The LSWR had to buy two 'A' class 0-6-0T engines from the London, Brighton & South Coast Railway to work it.

London
A resort? Yes, if you are one of the four-fifths of the British population who do not live in its urban, suburban and orbital sprawl. Inconveniently situated in a corner of the country, in a damp, airless, marshy valley, its attractions are not natural ones. Its position of capital city was nobody's plan, but was crystallized by the time King William I built the castle now known as the Tower, and has been retained ever since by the inertia engendered by its size. It should be remembered that during the 'ACE' period it was the biggest city in the world. If you wanted to see acres of famous specimens of architecture, shops where the newest and best of everything could be obtained, theatres where the biggest stars performed, museums where the most expensive works of art were reverently displayed, and the abbey church where monarchs have been crowned for 10 centuries, you had to come here. Tourists might not cross the world to see a little fishing port, but they all want to see with their own eyes the façades behind which the Empire was governed, and hear at first hand that quite unmelodious clang of Big Ben which is replayed all over the world and says, as much as the words, 'This is London'.

Nine Elms terminus, named after a nearby house, was built, as was usual for the time, as a traffic interchange with the River Thames, and was well outside London. Waterloo Bridge station (renamed Waterloo in 1886) was convenient for the centres of attraction for the visitor, as was confirmed right at the end of the 'ACE' era by its choice as the terminal for Continental trains. It received a boost in 1951 from the Festival of Britain held just across the road, and the building of the Royal Festival Hall, but the fact remains that the environs were near-slums, are brutal office blocks and aggressively anti-pedestrian roads, and nearly all the people you will see are there only because they are trying to get to somewhere else.

Left: Sidmouth terminus on 30 September 1964. The engine shed had not been used by the railway for some years. *J. Gready/ E.W.J. Crawforth Collection*

Left: Seaton station, by the mouth of the River Axe, lovely on a summer day. 'M7' No 30667 (numbered 30106 until 1961) sets off on another run to the junction on 26 August 1962. *K.A. Stone/ E.W.J. Crawforth Collection*

Below: Lyme Regis station on 12 June 1956, seen from near the engine shed. The 'ACE' coach is berthed in the bay platform. *E.W.J. Crawforth Collection*

7

Miscellanea

As noted earlier, the 'ACE' stopped at an unstaffed halt. This was Maddaford Moor, opened on 27 July 1926 on the site of a passing loop which had been removed in 1919. Trains stopped with the rear coach alongside the short platform. Its situation differed little from that of the next station, Ashbury; it served a district and was located conveniently for a road. There was no settlement near it except for a row of railway houses, one of which was still occupied by the last signalman's daughter 70 years after the box closed.

The passage of Southern and Western trains, both heading in the up or down sense (ie towards or away from London), through Exeter and Plymouth in opposite directions is well known, but less often remarked is that it also applied at two other stations. One was Mutley, the wooden station right at the end of Plymouth North Road's shunting neck, which was dismantled in March 1939. The other was Lydford, and from there to near Wilminstone Siding the double-track Southern line and the Great Western single track ran together without any connection. At Brentor station (SR) the Western track went past the back of the up platform and at Mary Tavy (GWR) the Southern line curved by in a cutting a few yards away. This ridiculous arrangement lasted until the lines closed.

The Southern, the world's busiest surface railway, had a safety record second to none, and it is a tribute to the men who ran it that the 'ACE' was not involved in any serious accidents. There was a collision on 8 August 1943 at Andover Junction, when the signalman decided to work a permanent-way motor trolley across the main line at the east end of the station while the up 'ACE' was approaching to stop there. He would have been all right, only the train overshot the platform and demolished the trolley. Fortunately, no one was near it at the time and there were no casualties. Such minor errors of judgement resulted from the stress and fatigue of four years of war.

Potentially more serious was the breaking of a tender axle on No 35023 *Holland-Afrika Line*, at Broad Clyst on the up train on 11 November 1954, but by good fortune again there was no other damage. The train was hauled back to Pinhoe, while Exmouth Junction hastily turned out a substitute engine, which took the train forward, passing the immobile casualty on the wrong line under emergency single-line regulations.

Incidents there were of course, such as the lucky escape of a guard in September 1947. He signalled his train away from Camelford, but in turning to look out after boarding the van he fell out onto the platform. He rushed out of the station and persuaded a car driver to take him up to Otterham, but there they were told that a passenger had seen his fall and pulled the communication chain, and the driver had stopped half a mile out. They therefore drove back to Camelford, whence the guard walked out to the train, which proceeded on its way an hour behind time.

The major Taw valley landowner was the Earl of Portsmouth, who, in return for admitting the railway, retained the right to have a station erected at the Portsmouth Arms Inn, and to stop trains there for his journeys between his rural responsibilities at Eggesford House and his State duties at Westminster. Right up till the war the 'ACE' had a stop scheduled to set down passengers from London or Salisbury on prior notice, and to pick them up for those destinations on notice being received before departure from Barnstaple. During the war the down train stopped at Eggesford for crossing purposes, but to preserve the image of a nonstop express the stop was unadvertised — a futile gesture.

The 'Merchant Navy' engine *Elders Fyffes* was popular at Exeter, because when she was booked to work in there a representative from the shipping line's local office would meet her and give the crew a bunch of bananas.

The 'ACE' made what later generations call a cross-platform interchange with a narrow gauge line, the Lynton & Barnstaple. In 1926 a train left Lynton at 9.2am, arriving at Barnstaple Town at 10.22. At 10.25 another little engine

would trundle round from the depot at Pilton; the first engine ran back light at 10.36, unless business was good enough to warrant its double-heading the train out at 10.45. Meanwhile the passengers were waiting for the up 'ACE' to arrive at 10.59. In the afternoon the down 'ACE' called at 3.40pm and the L&B train left at 4.5. In 1932 the morning connection was tighter, leaving Lynton at 9.25am and reaching Barnstaple at 10.56 with only 10min to wait for the bigger train, but incoming travellers had to hang around until 4.30pm. The L&B closed on 29 September 1935.

Connection was made with several bus services of the Devon General, Southern National and Western National companies, in which the Southern Railway had large holdings. The principal ones were: Exeter to Chagford in the Teign Valley, Barnstaple Junction to Lynton (vice the L&B), Braunton to Croyde, Ilfracombe to Combe Martin, Bideford to Appledore, Westward Ho! and Clovelly, Bude to Stratton and Widemouth Bay, Camelford to Tintagel and Boscastle, Wadebridge to Newquay, Padstow to Bedruthan and Trevone Bay, Seaton to Beer and Lyme Regis to Charmouth. These connections were important, and in prewar summers the stops at Braunton, Bideford and Camelford were extended to up to 5min instead of the usual 1min or 2min.

Right up to the end the Southern Region operated a 'ticket interavailability' scheme with the bus companies, and in particular on winter Sundays and other times when no trains ran on the Padstow, Seaton and Lyme Regis lines, railway tickets were valid for the bus services and vice versa. Note that the railway fares were higher than the bus fares, and passengers using a bus ticket on a train had to pay the difference.

In those days connections were actually honoured, between trains and trains and between trains and buses.

There were many other bus operators who competed with the trains, and it is surely no coincidence that one named Hardy-Colwills of Barnstaple took large press advertisements for an enhanced service to Bideford commencing on 19 July 1926.

The Plymouth 'ACE' came nearer to boxing the compass than any other train in Britain. After running southwest into Exeter, at Cowley Bridge box its nose was pointing due north. It described a huge arc around Dartmoor until it was coming down the Tavy valley, heading southeast near Double Waters, west by north at Bere Alston, and due east as it passed under the GW line at St Budeaux. From south-southwest at Ford, it swung round through Devonport to northeast, then circled Plymouth to arrive at Friary station aligned just about due west.

People on board the Torrington and Ilfracombe portions could watch the other train running parallel on the far side of the Taw estuary. As the one was emerging from the cutting to cross Fremington Pill, the other was coming round the curve through Wrafton. Similarly, by the time the first down portion had finished its business at Barnstaple Town and was starting along the north side, the second one was setting forth from the Junction along the south side.

Left: Summer in the Exe valley. 'T9' No 30717 is brought forward from the Cowley Bridge Junction home signal with the 2.33pm from Plymouth on 22 August 1959. This engine is clearly having a busy time, indicated by the patch on the smokebox where the paint has been burnt off by hot ash accumulating inside. *S.C. Nash*

Right: Camelford, alighting point for the Arthurian legend. On 24 June 1949, No 31834 with the afternoon down freight has shunted into the up loop to allow the 'ACE' to pass. *S.C. Nash/ E.W.J. Crawforth Collection*

In the writer's view, the most interesting parts of a railway are where it leaves its fenced enclaves and joins the rest of us on roadway and quayside. The first level crossing was 90 miles from London, an uncontrolled occupation crossing on a farm drive near Barford St Martin. The first manned crossing was at Teffont Mill, on the lane leading to the mill on the River Nadder. There were 17 more on the way to Exeter, most on comparatively unfrequented roads, except those at the stations of Sherborne, Chard Junction, Sidmouth Junction and Pinhoe. Outdoing these, the most extraordinary level crossing anywhere, was Red Cow Crossing (named after the adjacent pub) at Exeter St David's. On an important road leading to one of Exeter's two bridges over the River Exe, it went through the middle of this vital piece of railway, crossing 14 tracks including the bank engine siding and the goods shed road, with three turnouts actually partially buried in the roadway. With conventional gates impossible, it was watched from Goods Yard signalbox and a keeper's hut below Middle box.

Crediton had three crossings in close proximity, but there was only one other, Lake Crossing, all the way to Plymouth. The North Devon had six, including the intriguingly-named Higher Doomsford Crossing. However, the Ilfracombe line had no fewer than 11 in a distance of 11 miles, and that was a real problem, the manning cost being eventually held to blame for the line's closure. The only ones on the Cornwall lines were Venn Gates up on Maddaford Moor, Halwill station, Egloskerry station, and Wadebridge, in the town centre, closing across the main A39 coast road.

The 'ACE' is not concerned with quay sidings, but it is worth mentioning that at Barnstaple, Fremington, Bideford, Bude, Wadebridge, Padstow, Devonport, Plymouth Friary and Exmouth, tracks branched off to bring wagons alongside boats. In 1991 the legend 'South Western Railway Offices' was still visible on the company's building above Plymouth's Sutton Pool, and a ridge in the tarmac by Padstow harbour leads one to suppose that the most southwesterly rails on the South Western might still be sleeping beneath it.

A reader who has not seen the rectangular headboard from close to, might be surprised by the size of it. It measures 50in by 15in. At the back are two large brackets to stand it clear of the smokebox door handle, with slots to sit it on the two door-mounted lamp brackets. On top are substitute lamp brackets. The originals are made of cast aluminium. It is not known how many were made, although the writer has seen at least four preserved examples.

The headboard was a BR innovation, and until about 1953 an even bigger device was used, measuring 5ft by 2ft, which sat on the front platform of the engine and had a hole in the middle for the centre bottom headlight to show through.

Both types of headboard could only be carried by Bulleid Pacifics, and from these they were frequently absent. This may be explained partly by the difficulty of having the boards to hand in the right places and putting them on and off engines which worked many different trains during their day's duties, and partly by the working railwayman's point of view that such embellishments were imposed by a distant head office. Their use was not mandatory and train names were never shown in the Working Timetables. Before the war, notwithstanding the prominence in publicity photographs of the expensive machine at the front of the train, engines wore no headboards — presumably on the grounds that the passengers would not see them and passers-by near the line would not be interested in the trains. After the war, although

Left: Typical of the North Devon stations is King's Nympton. At that time, July 1980, the house was in private occupation. *SHA*

Below left: Lynton & Barnstaple Railway engine No 762 running round its train at Barnstaple Town station.
E.W.J. Crawforth Collection

Above right: The later headboard, on No 35029 *Ellerman Lines* passing Brookwood. Close inspection shows a Tavern Car, fourth vehicle. The Saturday train numbers were lashed on in various amateurish ways.
J.H. Owen/MNLPS Collection

Bottom: Red Cow level crossing, Exeter St David's; an extraordinary thing to have in the middle of the busiest station in the entire West Country. The attendant is standing on the bank engine siding. (1962)
Ian Allan Library

the coaches were kept spotless, the management interest in the appearance of the engine declined steadily; there was no incentive from above shed level to smarten it up and use the headboard, and it was a tribute to the dedication of the men that any cleaning was done at all. Salisbury and Exmouth Junction depots had a reputation for well-kept engines.

Coach roof boards were important in directing passengers to the correct part of the train, and were always scrupulously applied. They were the responsibility of the station staff, except in the case of Waterloo, for which they were fitted at Clapham Yard.

On the Southern Railway and Region the white discs or headlamps on the engine indicated the route of the train. The available positions were: 1, at the top; 2 and 3 on the smokebox front; 4, 5 and 6 along the bottom. The codes were: Waterloo–Plymouth 1 and 5; Exeter–Ilfracombe 1; Barnstaple Junction–Torrington 3; Exeter–Padstow 2 and 3; Halwill–Bude 3; Sidmouth Junction–Sidmouth 2; Tipton–Exmouth 5; Seaton Junction–Seaton 3; Axminster–Lyme Regis 5; Yeovil Junction–Yeovil Town 3; Waterloo–Clapham empty trains 4 and 6. The engine duty number was pasted on one of the discs. Although in theory these arrangements would enable the train to be identified, in practice, especially in places where the only railwaymen about were local men who knew what was going on, they were not always rigorously applied.

The reader should not think that any aspect of running the 'ACE' was allowed to be haphazard. Take the supply of towels in the lavatories. They were put in before starting, four in each First and three in each Third, and removed at the end of the run. Used ones were sent once a week from each subsidiary station to its concentration point in a hamper with a memorandum showing the number sent. Every Wednesday morning the subsidiary stations were to telegraph their supply requirements to the concentration points, which in turn advised their Divisional Superintendent, who ordered supplies from the Towel Depot, Waterloo Junction. Stations had to record and return: number of clean towels on hand at 10am each Wednesday, number issued the previous week, number required for the next week, and numbers of soiled and condemned towels sent to the concentration point in the previous week. The subsidiary stations were Clapham Junction, Wimbledon Park, Walton, Woking, Lyme Regis, Seaton, Sidmouth, Exmouth, Okehampton, Bude, Launceston, Padstow, Barnstaple Junction and Torrington. The concentration points were Waterloo, Salisbury, Yeovil, Exeter Central, Plymouth Friary and Ilfracombe. (From the 1934 General Appendix.)

Tower Hill achieved the melancholy distinction of being the only station west of Exeter to have its living accommodation demolished after closure, and that was by a 'sort of' accident. The new owner engaged a contractor to demolish the subsidiary structures and tidy up. Next weekend he found the house razed to rubble, and the site has lain empty ever since.

All the stations had their individualities and landmarks, but as this is about the train not the track, we will mention just one particular favourite: the monkey-puzzle tree in the station house's garden at Whimple. It was there before the 1923 amalgamation, and was still standing defiantly out of the dereliction when the writer checked it in 1993.

Although it is going outside our period, it was on Pentire Head near Padstow that poet Laurence Binyon composed *For the Fallen*, the lines which have become the national lament for those who gave their lives for their country. It is a tribute that such inspiration should come from this noble coastline, and a fine termination to a journey on the 'Atlantic Coast Express'.

Left: No account of the burgeoning of the Atlantic Coast service would be complete without the famous photograph of young Ronald Witt, so here is our version. This was the inspiration for the 'Summer comes Soonest in the South' slogan. In the photo, but omitted from the subsequent artist's versions, was Waterloo A signalbox. *MNLPS Collection*

Below: Salisbury Cathedral is visible to the driver, but sadly not the passengers, when approaching from the west. No 35007 *Aberdeen Commonwealth* in 1954. *G.F. Heiron*

8 The Legend Lives On

The typical West Country topographical book of the first quarter of the 20th century was written by someone of the leisured classes, who extolled the beauty of the country and the antiquity of its churches, and desired them to be enjoyed by only a few persons of the same class as themselves. Here is one A.G. Folliot-Stokes in 1912: 'At present there is no railroad parallel with this coast between Tintagel and Hartland. Soon, however, the LSW or the GWR will surely run a line between these two points, and then goodbye to the spirit of the Wild and the creatures of the Wild. But the cliffs and coves and the wild fury of the Atlantic will remain. Thank God, no number of trippers can destroy them.'

Another writer in 1912, a Rev Breton, described Calstock as 'spoilt' by the viaduct and regarded Tintagel's distance from the station as an advantage — it 'kept away the tripper element'. He also claimed, by the way, that in the early days of the North Cornwall Railway a 'very big navvy' sat on the front buffer-beam of the engine to open gates. Since there are only two level crossings on the route, we wonder of what gates he was thinking.

In 1925 another such writer, V.C. Clinton-Baddeley, referred to the prospect of a railway from Bideford to Clovelly, Hartland and Bude, but did not think it likely that any railway would venture into the uplands south of Torrington, apparently unaware that the North Devon & Cornwall Junction Light Railway was just being completed. He or she saw most of Devon as little developed outside the main resorts and unlikely to change. Apparently a witch-doctor was brought to court in Exeter in 1903, which is really pretty recent.

Left: In the 1930s, when no shed would dream of handing out grubby disc boards and no adult would step out without putting on a hat. Gleaming 'N15s' wait to leave Waterloo, No 751 *Etarre* on the 4.50pm Portsmouth and No 777 *Sir Lamiel* on the 5pm Exeter. *G.J. Jefferson*

Such exclusive doctrine was anathema to the Southern Railway, which wanted as many people as possible to enjoy the countryside, using its trains. Around the year 1930 it began running Sunday excursions specifically directed at young Londoners bound for country rambles, and was overwhelmed by the response. It now engaged S.P.B. Mais, a popular writer and broadcaster on rural topics, to write holiday and walking guides in his robust and, for the time, racy style. Mais, who also wrote for the other railways, aligned his material to suit his customers. While the Great Western Visitor was a scholar of ancient history, proceeding from one church screen to the next, the Southern Rambler was a lover of the open spaces and the life of the village. The important task of conveying the idea that Southern resorts were tremendously popular because they were never crowded, was carried through with a masterly touch.

He started with *Southern Rambles for Londoners*, a guide to walks just outside the then limit of the suburban area, then *Walking at Week Ends*, rather further afield. Then came *Let's Get Out Here*, 'an account of twenty-six walks from points on the route of the Atlantic Coast Express'. The walks were in areas around Salisbury, Sherborne, Seaton, Okehampton, Tavistock and Padstow. Finally, there were 10 more in the Barnstaple area in *Walks in North Devon*.

They are as valuable now as when they were written, but reading them from the standpoint of 60 years later is a bittersweet experience. One profound change is of course that you must in most cases arrive on your ground by car. Many of his ways are overgrown, fenced off or built over, and the lanes he described, in those days untarred and unfrequented, are no longer safe to walk. On the other hand, the footpath network is often better, and many spots are quite heart-wrenchingly the same as they were then, so on the cliffs or moors, once you are well away from the road, you can still enjoy what was as important a part of the 'ACE' as the train ride.

On the subject of the train journey, the Southern's version of the popular 'Route book'

was an unusual and delightful piece. Called simply *A C E*, it combined Mais's text with a swirling torrent of drawings by Anna Zinkeisen. Much of it referred to the obligatory battles, kings and bishops of the Middle Ages, but looking through it we see also a highwayman, a World War 1 tank, smugglers, Barnstaple Fair and a typical 1930s bathing-suited beauty on a surfboard. As a commentary on, largely, the non-railway aspects of the route, it cannot be bettered.

During the war production of such material was progressively curtailed, but it was only in 1943 that restrictions really began to bite. An aspect which looks most poignant in hindsight is that the January 1940 Public Timetable makes no reference whatsoever to the war until the back page, where there is an advertisement for the *Hints For Holidays 1940*: 'For a change of scene and air in these trying times'.

The British Railways holiday guides were pretty much an expression of a hope that things would resume as they had left off when war intervened, and embodied the same air of gentility, which by the late 1950s was looking more and more out of touch. In the 1957 edition we read of 'a popular little watering-place' (Trevone), 'a place of uncommon charm' (Launceston), 'a pleasant place in which to linger' (Okehampton), or Boscastle 'beloved of those who seek a refuge from the rush and bustle of modern existence'. Sidmouth was 'Recommended by the Medical Profession', while Exmouth bravely described itself as 'the English Bay of Naples'. The hotels gave their 'terms' in guineas and emphasised that they had hot and cold water and interior-sprung mattresses.

Hardly the sort of thing to appeal to the new breed of vigorous youth with time and money to spare.

Above: A classic location, the lower reach of Honiton Bank where the line curves away from the Axe valley. This is the Saturday 9am down on 23 July 1962; engine No 35012 *United States Lines. Dr I. Wood*

A new approach was needed, and was partially achieved with leaflets and posters groping towards the bold, even stark, presentation associated with the 1960s. It was not until 1962 that a really populist approach was seen in the brochure *Want to Run a Railway?*, which addressed the reader as 'Mate' and committed the crashing bloomer of saying that the railway put its equipment to more use in a day than it was built to stand in a year — implying that either the designers or the buyers were staggeringly incompetent. This was aimed at commuters, because by then the British Railways Board had decided that holiday travellers were not an economic source of revenue.

It is sad but true that if we take an assessment based on what appears in literature aimed at people who are not interested in railways, which means nearly everyone, the 'ACE' comes off very badly. Most modern books will unbend for half a page or so to admit that the Great Western Railway was regarded with some affection by the travelling public, but the Southern Railway is mentioned not at all. Even those contemporary publishers that made an effort were markedly ill-informed. A guide to Cornwall printed in 1946 remarked of Padstow that, 'The S. Western Railway Co are spending great sums of money in perfecting the fish dock'. It does, however, mention that the visitor is served by the 'comforts of the Atlantic Coast and

Above: Let's Get Out Here, a copy from 1937, and the earlier *Southern Rambles.* shown along with *Walking at Week-ends* and *Walks in North Devon*. *C.J. Austin*

Below: The cover of *ACE* has a plastic window and a country view on the next page. *C.J. Austin*

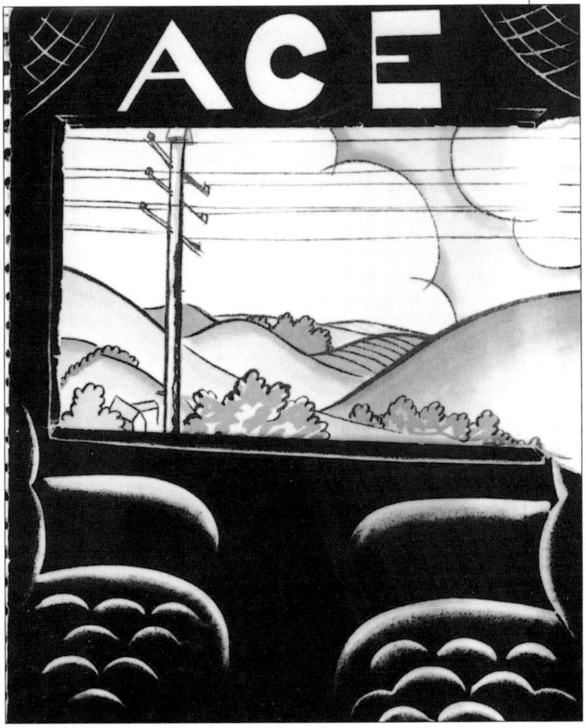

Below: The drawings in *ACE* were printed in red and blue, as were the place names in the text according to whether they were on the left or the right of the down train. The viaduct dashingly rendered on this page is not Meldon as implied by the text, but perhaps resembles Shillamill. *C.J. Austin*

The next thirty miles down to Plymouth is probably the finest panorama of England obtainable from any railway carriage window, and indeed you will at times find yourself comparing it with the Western Highlands.

No sooner is Okehampton left behind than we see the vast granite quarries of MELDON, whence comes the material for all the bridges we have passed over.

The stone quarried from here also goes to make those concrete fence posts that border the line, the cable posts and the new platform coping slabs on the stations.

This huge quarry covers eighty acres and contains four million cubic yards of first-grade stone. The working face is over a quarter of a mile long and about 140 feet high. The average annual output of this great quarry is six thousand cubic yards of rubble stone, eighty-two thousand cubic yards of 2½ in. ballast, thirteen thousand cubic yards of one-inch ballast and sixteen thousand cubic yards of chippings.

Just beyond the quarries we pass over MELDON VIADUCT, below which fall the peat-brown waters of the West Okement down a wild rugged ravine of granite boulders and bracken-covered sides. This is a combe of great beauty and gives promise of the finer beauties waiting to be discovered by those who have the heart to penetrate to the heart of the moor. The rough ground is a forest of wild holly trees rising above the bracken. The line for North Cornwall forks off to the north-west here, and we turn sharply south and begin the long descent of the Tamar Valley.

We are actually on the open moor at last and quickly rush past the church and hamlet of Sourton on the west.

41

Cornish Riviera Express's', and that is the only reference to the 'ACE' which the writer has found in a non-railway book.

Poor old King Arthur has not fared too well either. At the beginning of the century all the patrons wanted was a good, romantic story. The dramatic approach reached its histrionic peak when in 1930 a millionaire businessman named Frederick Thomas Glasscock came to Tintagel. He commissioned the building of a grand Hall of Chivalry, with a round table, paintings, robes, masses of fake heraldry, etc, and began knighting people — for a suitable fee. More sites in the Arthurian story were discovered, including one at Slaughter Bridge, which by an amazing coincidence was only a few yards from Camelford station!

However, in mid-century a harsh cynicism took over, with most authorities satisfying themselves that the whole saga was a fact-free nonsense. A lot of other things lost their romance for a lot of people about then, including trains. As we approach the end of the century, the desire is for scrupulous scholarship, and the presentations at Tintagel and elsewhere explain with friendly honesty what is known and what merely guessed. It is sad that the quest for truth rules out the magic, chivalry and shining armour; as perhaps it does the immaculate, impeccably operated train dedicated to nothing but the service of an appreciative community. Their more enduring value may be as ideals towards which to strive.

Could Waterloo to the West of England have survived? Whatever your views on the historical perspective, the writer would argue there were three prerequisites for it to have had a chance.

It would have had to accept the seasonal nature of its business, follow the example of the independent railways, and change the rigid demarcation of its staffing to a multi-skilled workforce, who were out operating the trains in summer and in the shops overhauling them in winter.

It should have made its public railway-conscious, by not only advertising its services but also making the railway an object of interest in itself, so that people would see it as an amenity rather than a mere utility. Again following the independent railways, it would have encouraged people to visit it and watch trains, and sold souvenirs, books about its equipment and operations, and so on. This the Southern did not attempt to do. It was an employee in the Public Relations Office who was so disgusted with the railway's flat refusal to disseminate information about itself, that he set up in business himself to satisfy this interest. His name was Ian Allan.

It would have needed investment, and by that we are talking not service subsidies, but major works and big money. No one thought of rebuilding the North Cornwall Railway to permit cruising speeds of up to 80mph, although that is what was done to the roads, serving places many of which were less populous in the 1980s than they were in the 1880s. A few million pounds spent here and there on the railway, easing alignments and bringing stations closer to the towns, would have made a difference. The tangles should have been sorted out; for example, Barnstaple should have been given back its waterfront in exchange for a direct line (proposed in 1884) from Bishop's Tawton to Victoria Road and on through where the ring road is now, rejoining the original route above Braunton. Halwill to Launceston should have been closed and replaced by a route via a triangular junction at Lydford and the uprated GW Launceston branch. Bodmin North and General should have been replaced by a through station, to accommodate a fast service on a Plymouth–Launceston–Padstow–Bodmin–Plymouth circuit. Junctions would have had to be rebuilt; for instance, Sidmouth Junction given an east to south curve, so that London trains could wheel through it and be at rest in the terminus in about 11min instead of 23. And of course, trains would be of multiple-unit type, in which joining and dividing is easy and the installed power is always matched to the train length.

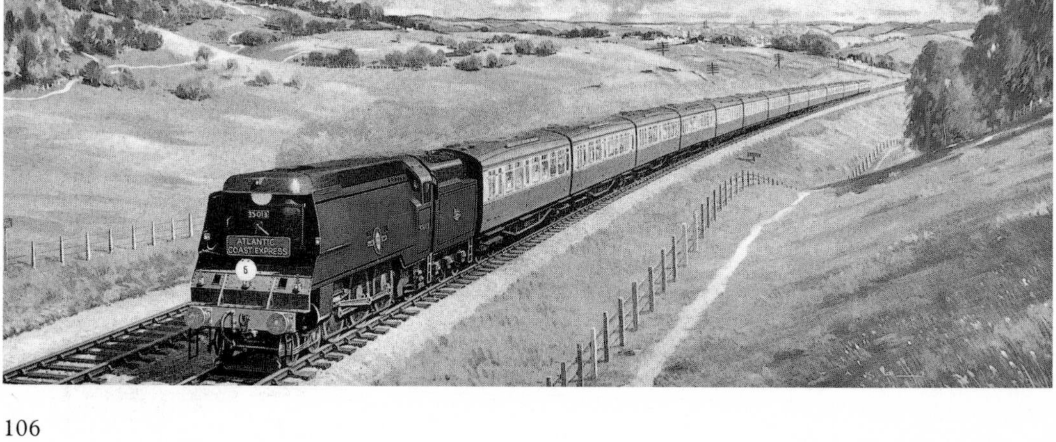

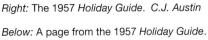

Right: The 1957 *Holiday Guide*. *C.J. Austin*

Below: A page from the 1957 *Holiday Guide*. *C.J. Austin*

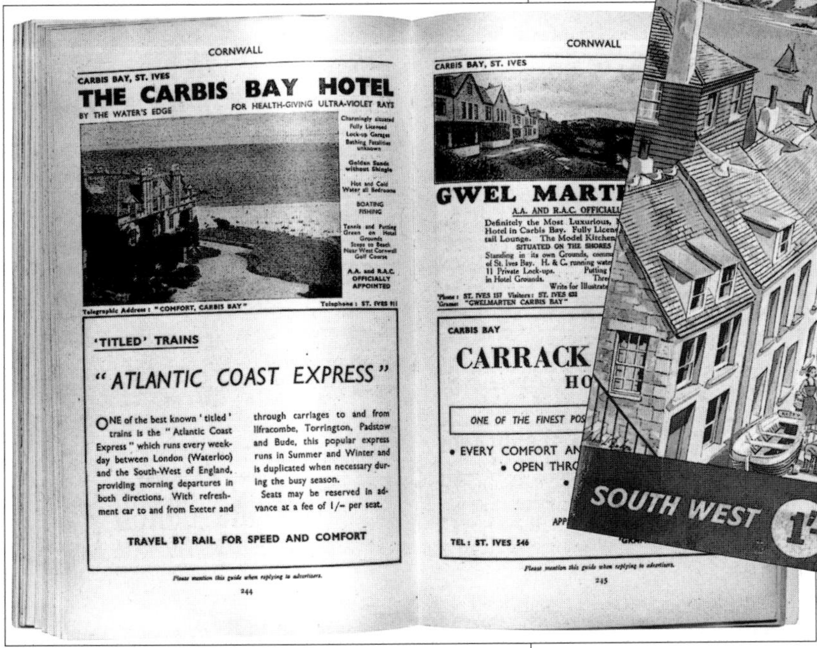

CORNWALL

CARBIS BAY, ST. IVES

THE CARBIS BAY HOTEL

BY THE WATER'S EDGE

FOR HEALTH-GIVING ULTRA-VIOLET RAYS

Charmingly situated
Fully Licensed
Lock-up Garages
Bathing Fatalities unknown

Golden Sands without Shingle

Hot and Cold Water all Bedrooms

BOATING
FISHING

Tennis and Putting Green on Hotel Grounds
Steps to Beach
Near West Cornwall Golf Course

A.A. and R.A.C. OFFICIALLY APPOINTED

Telegraphic Address: "COMFORT, CARBIS BAY" Telephone: ST. IVES 911

'TITLED' TRAINS

"ATLANTIC COAST EXPRESS"

ONE of the best known 'titled' trains is the "Atlantic Coast Express" which runs every week-day between London (Waterloo) and the South-West of England, providing morning departures in both directions. With refreshment car to and from Exeter and through carriages to and from Ilfracombe, Torrington, Padstow and Bude, this popular express runs in Summer and Winter and is duplicated when necessary during the busy season.

Seats may be reserved in advance at a fee of 1/- per seat.

TRAVEL BY RAIL FOR SPEED AND COMFORT

Please mention this guide when replying to advertisers.

244

CORNWALL

CARBIS BAY, ST. IVES

GWEL MARTE…

A.A. AND R.A.C. OFFICIALL…

Definitely the Most Luxurious, … Hotel in Carbis Bay. Fully Licen… tail Lounge. The Model Kitchen…
SITUATED ON THE SHORES …
Standing in its own Grounds, comm… of St. Ives Bay. H. & C. running wat… 11 Private Lock-ups. Putting … in Hotel Grounds. Thre…
Write for Illustrat…

'Phone: ST. IVES 157 Visitors: ST. IVES 621
'Grams: "GWELMARTEN CARBIS BAY"

CARBIS BAY

CARRACK …
HO…

ONE OF THE FINEST POS…

• EVERY COMFORT AN…
• OPEN THRO…

APP…

TEL: ST. IVES 546

Please mention this guide when replying to advertisers.

245

Left: This painting was placed in the bulkhead display panels in coaches and its design, 'from a watercolour by Richard Ward', is simplified for impact. It depicts a blue 'Merchant Navy' with red and cream stock. The location is clearly supposed to be East Devon, although pink earth is not peculiar to that county. *Courtesy of the Southern Coach Preservation Group*

Above: Devon and Cornish Days by E.P. Leigh-Bennet discribed various locations in the West country, along with a map of the route of the ACE and contained paintings by L. Richmond. *Robert Antell Collection*

Below: The Summer 1947 Timetable. It uses two shades of green and sunshine yellow lettering in the upper half. The winter timetables were more sombre, in dark green and white jackets. *C.J. Austin*

Left: In the Kensey Valley is found the only part of the 'ACE' route where scheduled steam-hauled trains still run: the Launceston Steam Railway carries on the tradition in a small but determined way. The engine is Quarry Hunslet *Lilian. SHA*

Below left: How many of the tourists who patronise the 'Shipwrights' in Padstow notice the concrete device by the wall? It is Milepost 259¼, the last but one on the line, which originally stood just outside the station near where a footpath crossed the track to give access to moorings on the river. Milepost 259½ stood by the station house. *Mrs J.E. Price*

However, if you are to become a legend it is arguably better to die young and tragically, and a 'Modernised ACE' would be about as romantic as King Arthur's knights driving delivery vans. Cornwall is a land of legends, and this brief flowering of railway travel is one more of them. It is not as massively popular as the King Arthur, Pisky & Cream Tea industry, but among its devotees it stands firm. For every thousand tourists who troop thorough Tintagel's arch and imagine Launcelot on a white horse, there is one elsewhere — listening to the wind in the grass below Sourton Tor or gazing up Little Petherick Creek. The mind hears the clang of the shovel, the whistle, the silence of the train easing into motion and the first beat from the chimney; and sees the white steam, the long green train and the oily, sulphurous steed bearing a proud name — 'ATLANTIC COAST EXPRESS'.

Below: The Camel Estuary; a view from Trevanson towards Padstow on 13 July 1989. This shows the river at its best, at high water under a cloudless sky. The vacant trackbed is in use as a public footpath. *SHA*

Appendices: Time Tables

J 64 WEEKDAYS Okehampton, Halwill, Bude, Bodmin, Padstow and Torrington Branch

DOWN (UP, Halwill to Torrington)			Scholars	Scholars		11.0 am or 11.5 am Waterloo			11.0 am Waterloo		LE		3.5 pm Plymouth North Road	Mixed		
			SX	SX										SX		
		PM	PM	PM	PM	PM	PM	PM	PM	PM	PM	PM	PM	PM	PM	PM
OKEHAMPTON .. arr	1					3 8			3 8							
.. dep	2					3 14			3 14		3‖50					
Meldon Jn.	3					3 22			3 22		3 58					
Maddaford Moor Halt	4															
Ashbury .. arr	5								3X32		4X10					
dep	6					3 30			3 33		4 17					
HALWILL .. arr	7					3 36			3 39		4‖23					
dep	8					3 39	3 43		3 43	3 47						
Dunsland Cross .. arr	9						3X49			3X53						
dep	10						3 50			3 54						
Holsworthy .. arr	11						3X58			4X 2						
dep	12						4 0			4 3						
Whitstone and arr	13						4 8			4 11						
Bridgerule dep	14						4 9			4 12						
BUDE .. arr	15						4 18			4 21						
Hole arr	16															
.. dep	17															
Hatherleigh arr	18															
.. dep	19															
Meeth Halt arr	20															
.. dep	21															
Petrockstow arr	22															
.. dep	23		Not advertised	Not advertised		Until 11th September inclusive	Until 11th September inclusive		Commences 14th September	Commences 14th September	Until 11th September inclusive			4 37		
Dunsbear Halt arr	24													4 46		
.. dep	25													4 47		
Yarde Halt arr	26													4 52		
.. dep	27													4 53		
Watergate Halt arr	28													5 6		
.. dep	29													5 7		
TORRINGTON .. arr	30													5 14		
Ashwater .. arr	31								3 50							
dep	32					3 45			3 51							
Tower Hill .. arr	33								3 57							
dep	34					3 50			3 58							
Launceston .. arr	35					3 56			4 5				4 39			
dep	36					3 59			4 8							
Egloskerry .. arr	37								4 16							
dep	38					4 6½			4 17							
Tresmeer .. arr	39								4X24							
dep	40					4 13½			4 25							
Otterham .. arr	41					4X23			4 34							
dep	42					4 24			4 35							
Camelford .. arr	43		Runs during School terms only	Runs during School terms only ECS or LE will run in this timing when scholars train not required	Terminate at Wadebridge until 11th September inclusive	4 31			4 42			Until 11th September inclusive		Conveys workmen		
dep	44					4 32			4 43							
Delabole .. arr	45					4 37			4 48							
dep	46					4 38			4 49							
Port Isaac Road .. arr	47					4 45			4X56							
dep	48					4 46			4 56½							
St. Kew Highway .. arr	49								5 0½							
dep	50					4 50			5 1							
BODMIN ROAD dep	51	2 30						4 25								
BODMIN arr	52	2 38						4 33								
GENERAL dep	53	2 49	4 8					4 50								
BODMIN NORTH dep	54				4 23										5 48	
Dunmere Halt	55				4 27										5 52	
Boscarne Jn.	56	2 55	4 14		4 28½			4 56							5 53½	
Nanstallon Halt	57		4 15½		4 30			4 57½							5 55	
Grogley Halt	58		4 20		4 34½										5 59½	
WADEBRIDGE .. arr	59	3 6	4 27½		4 42	4 56		5 9	5X 8						6 7	
dep	60			4 30	4 44	4 58			5 12			5 33				6 13
PADSTOW .. arr	61			4 39	4 53	5 7			5 21			5 42				6 22

Working Time Table 20 June 1959. *Author's Collection.*

DOWN

Station		No.	ECS		To Padstow and Bude		1.45 pm Exmouth	11.5 am Waterloo to Padstow and Bude					2.15 pm Exmouth	LE to Halwill	SX	SO	
			PM		PM		PM	PM	PM		PM		PM	PM	PM	PM	PM
SALISBURY	arr	1						12 32									
	dep	2						12 37									
Wilton South		3															
Dinton		4															
Tisbury		5															
Semley		6															
Gillingham		7															
TEMPLECOMBE	arr	8															
	dep	9															
Milborne Port		10															
Sherborne		11															
YEOVIL JN.	arr	12															
	dep	13						1 18									
Sutton Bingham		14															
Crewkerne		15															
Chard Jn.	arr	16															
	dep	17															
Axminster	arr	18						1 41									
	dep	19						1 42							1 55	1 55	1 55
SEATON JN.	arr	20													2 1	2 1	2 1
	dep	21													2 2	2 2	2 2
Honiton		22													2a18	2a18	2a18
SIDMOUTH JN.	arr	23													2 25	2 25	2 25
	dep	24													2 26	2 26	2‡31
Whimple		25													2 32½	2 32½	2 37½
Broad Clyst		26													2a39	2a39	2a44
Pinhoe		27													2a44	2a44	2a49
Exmouth Jn.		28					2 8	2 13					2 37		2 48	2 48	2 53
St. James' Park Halt		29					2a10½									2 50	
EXETER CENTRAL	arr	30			2 5		2 12	2 16					2 40		2 51	2 52	2 56
	dep	31			2 21			2 21									
Exeter St. Davids	arr	32			2 24			2 24									
	dep	33			2 27			2 27									
Cowley Bridge Jn.		34			2 30			2 30									
Newton St. Cyres		35															
Crediton		36															
YEOFORD	arr	37															
	dep	38															
Coleford Jn.		39			2 44			2 44									
Bow		40															
North Tawton		41			2a56			2a56									
Sampford Courtenay		42						3 8									
OKEHAMPTON	arr	43			3 8			3 14									
	dep	44			3 14			3 22	3 22					3‖50			
Quarry Halt		45															
Meldon Jn.		46			3 22				3 30					3 58			
Bridestowe		47							3 35½								
Lydford		48							3 42								
Brentor		49							3 45½								
TAVISTOCK NORTH		50							3a54½		4 25						
Bere Alston	arr	51									4 35½						
	dep	52									4 36½						
Bere Ferrers		53									4a42½						
Tamerton Foliot Halt		54									4 47						
St. Budeaux, Victoria Road		55	3† 45								4a52						
Ford		56									4c57						
Devonport, Kings Road		57	3 50						4a21		5g 4						
Devonport Jn.		58	3 52						4 23		5 6						
PLYMOUTH	arr	59							4 25		5 8						
NORTH ROAD	dep	60	3 54						4†27		5† 9						
Lipson Jn.		61	3 58						4 31		5 13						
Mount Gould Jn.		62	3 59						4 32		5 14						
Friary Jn.		63	3 59½						4 32½		5 14½						
PLYMOUTH FRIARY	arr	64	4† 2						4†35		5†17						
Copplestone		65															
Morchard Road		66															
Lapford		67															
Eggesford		68															
Kings Nympton		69															
Portsmouth Arms		70															
Umberleigh		71															
Chapelton		72															
Barnstaple, Victoria Rd.	arr	73															
	dep	74															
BARNSTAPLE JN.	arr	75															
	dep	76															
Barnstaple Town		77															
Pottington Box		78															
Wrafton		79															
Braunton		80															
Mortehoe and Woolacombe		81															
ILFRACOMBE	arr	82															
Fremington		83															
Instow		84															
Bideford Goods		85															
Bideford		86															
TORRINGTON	arr	87															

ECS column: Until 11th September inclusive

To Padstow and Bude column: Will not run when 11.5 am Waterloo to Padstow runs

11.5 am Waterloo to Padstow and Bude column: MFO until 17th July inclusive. Mondays to Fridays 20th July to 4th September, 7th and 11th September and G

LE to Halwill column: Until 11th September inclusive

SX column: Commencing 14th September

Last column: Until 11th September inclusive

Working Time Table 20 June 1959. *Author's Collection.*

From WATERLOO to THE WEST OF ENGLAND—Weekdays

Miles from London	Station		p.m	a.m	a.m	a.m	a.m	a.m	a.m	a.m	a.m	a.m	a.m	a.m	a.m	a.m	a.m	a.m	a.m	p.m	a.m	p.m	p.m	a.m	a.m	a.m	a.m		p.m	noon		p.n
	324 WATERLOO	dep	10Z30		1 25													5 40	7 20	—	9 0					9 30	10 50			12 0		
	324 Surbiton	"	10Z13															5 59	7 38		9U17					9U48						
	324 Woking	"	11Z6															6 30	7 57		9 35					10 6						
48	Basingstoke	dep	11Z51															7 31	8 48		10 8					1045						
52¾	Oakley																	7 42	8 59							1054						
55¾	Overton																	7 48	9 5							11 0						
59½	Whitchurch A																	7 56	9 11							11 6						
61¼	Hurstbourne																	8 1	9 16							1111						
66½	Andover Junction 376				2 54													8 15	9 28		1036					1121						
72¼	Grateley																	8 27	9 40							1131						
78¼	Porton 356		a.m															8 38	9 51							1142						
83¾	SALISBURY 339, 356, 376	arr	2 36		3 18													8 48	10 2		11 1					1152	12 33					
		dep	2 42		3 24	3 35											8 0	9 30			11 5				1115		12 33					
86¼	Wilton B					3 43											8 7	9 36							1121							
92	Dinton																8 17	9 46							1131							
96¼	Tisbury					4 3											8 26	9 54							1139							
101½	Semley					4 15											8 38	10 7							1149							
105¼	Gillingham (Dorset)		3 23			4 24											8 48	1020							1157							
112¼	Templecombe		3 36			4 41									7 15	8 45	9B12	1032			1143			1158	1212							
114¾	Millborne Port					4 48									7 20	8 51	9 18	Stop						12 4	1220							
118¼	Sherborne		3 50			4 58									7 26	8 58	9 25				1157			1211	1229							
123	Yeovil Junction 355	arr	4 3			5 8									7 35	9 7	9 33				12 5			1219	1240							
124¾	355 Yeovil (Town)	arr	4 17			5 23									7 40	9 16	9 47				1216			1257	1257							
		dep				Stop							6 25		Stop	Stop	9 28				1155			1155								
—	Yeovil Junction	dep											6 31				9 39				12 6			1222								
125¼	Sutton Bingham																9 46							1228								
131¾	Crewkerne												6 46				9 58							1239								
134¾	Chard Junction 355	arr											7 0				1012							1252								
143	355 Chard	arr											8 37				11 6							1 2[illegible]								
		dep															9 34							1210								
—	Chard Junction	dep											7 1				1015		Stop					1254								
144¾	Axminster 355	arr											7 9				1024				1235			[illegible]								
151½	355 Lyme Regis	arr											8 56		a.m		11 4				1 18			2 14								
		dep													7J20		10 0				1134			1229					1SO24			
—	Axminster	dep											7 11		7 55		1027				1236			1 4					2SO2			
148	Seaton Junction 355	arr											7 18		8 1		1034				1243			1 11					2SO8			
152½	355 Seaton	arr											8 17		8 17		1052				1 5			2 2								
		dep													7 46		10 5				1228			1228					1 20			
—	Seaton Junction	dep											7 20		8 2		1035				1244			1 13					2 10			
155	Honiton												7 36		8 18		1052							1 30					2 26			
159½	Sidmouth Junc. 356	arr											7 43		8 25		11 0				1 6			[illegible]			2 8		2 34	3 16		
167¾	356 Sidmouth	arr											8 24		8 52		1135				1 32			2 49			2 48		3D43	3 43		
171	356 Budleigh Salter'n	"											9 23		9 23		1144				1 50			3			3 3					
175¾	356 Exmouth	"											9 37		9 37	a.m	1156				2 3			3 17			3 17					
—	356 Sidmouth	dep											7 20			1020	1020				1234			1234			1 35		1 35			
—	Sidmouth Junction	dep											7 45		8 26	1047	11 2				[illegible]			1 40			2 11		2 35	3 18		
16[illegible]¼	Whimple												7 52		8 32	1054				1 0			1 34	1 47					2 42			
167	Broad Clyst												7 59		8 38	11 1				1 5			1 39	1 54					2 48			
169	Pinhoe												8 4		8 43	11 6				1 10			1 44	1 59					2 53			
171¾	EXETER Central 357	arr			5 13								8 12		8 50	1114	1119			1 18	1 24		1 51	2 7			2 29		3 2	3 36		
182¼	357 Exmouth	arr			7 10								8 39		9 44	12 7	12 7	a.m		2 0	2 [illegible]			3 12			3 12		4L26	4L26		
		dep				a.m						6 40	7 45	8 10	Stop	Stop	1045	1045		Stop	1215	1215					1 30	1 30	Stop	2 45	2 45	
—	EXETER Central	dep			5 20	5 31						7 35	8 20	8 40			1127	1146			1 32	1 44					2 34	2 46		3 39	3 48	
72¼	Exeter (St. David's)				5 25	5 39						7 44	8 26	8 47			1135	1153			1A41	1 49					2 41	2 51		3 45	3 52	
76¾	Newton St. Cyres											7 54	8 36					12 3				1 58										
79	Crediton					5 52						8 0	8 42	9 1			1148	1211			1 54	2 4										
183	Yeoford	arr				6 0						8 8	8 50	9 9			1156	1219				2 12										
			1	2	3	4	5	6	7	8	9	10	11	12	13	14	15	16	17	18	19	20	21	22	23	24	25	26	27	28	29	30

Column 1: Via Eastleigh. Tuesday to Saturday mornings. Stop.

Column 11: Calls at St. James' Park Halt at 8 10 a.m.

Column 17: Calls at Idmiston Halt at 9 48 a.m.

Column 18: Saturdays only. Calls at St. James' Park Halt at 1 15 p.m.

Column 21: Saturdays excepted.

Column 24: Calls at Idmiston Halt at 11 39 a.m.

Column 25: Atlantic Coast Express. Refreshment Car, London to Exeter. Through Carriages to Seaton, Sidmouth and Exmouth.

Column 27: Calls at St. James' Park Halt at 2 59 p.m on Saturdays.

Column 28: Devon Belle. Mondays, Fridays and Saturdays. Runs until 27th October, 1947.

Public Time Table 6 October 1947. *Author's Collection.*

Miles	Station	1	2	3	4	5	6	7	8	9	10	11	12	13	14	15
—	**Yeoford** dep				6 1						8 9		9 11			
187¾	Bow										8 17		9 21			
191	North Tawton										8 24		9 28			
93¾	Sampford Courtenay										8 31		9 35			
197¾	Okehampton arr	a.m			6 23						8 40		9 44			
—	**Okehampton** dep	4 23									8 43		9 46			
204	Bridestowe										9 0		10 2			
207¼	Lydford										9 7		1010			
208¾	Brentor										9 11		1014			
213¾	Tavistock **C**	4 55	6 0	6P55					7 58	8 44	9 21		1026			
220½	Bere Alston 357		6 13					7 53	8 11	8 55	9 33		1043			
223	Bere Ferrers		6 21					7 59		Stop	9 39		1050			
225	Tamerton Foliot		6 26					8 4			9 44		1055			
227½	St. Budeaux, for Saltash		6 31					8 9	8 26		9 49		11 0			
228¾	Ford (Devon)		6 35					8 13	8 32		9 53		11 4			
229¾	**Devonport D** arr		6 39	7 31				8 17	8 36		9 57		11 8			
230¼	**PLY-** North Rd. "		6 43	7 36				8 23	8 43		10 5		1114			
234	**MOUTH** Friary "		6 54	7 48				8 33	8 55		1016		1125			
—	**Yeoford** dep			Stop		6 10		Stop	Stop			8 51				1157
186	Copplestone					6 18						8 57				12 4
187½	Morchard Road					6 22						9 1				12 8
190	Lapford					6 27						9 6				1213
193¾	Eggesford **F**					6 34				a.m		9 14				1221
197¾	South Molton Road **G**					6 41				8 28		9 21				1229
200¾	Portsmouth Arms					6 47				8 33		9 29				1235
204¼	Umberleigh					6 54				8 40		9 37				1242
207¼	Chapelton									8 45		9 42				1247
211½	**Barnstaple Junc. H** arr					7 4		a.m		8 52		9 49		a.m		1254
	Barnstaple Junc. H dep					7 15		8 0		Stop		9 59		1113		1 0
212¼	**Barnstaple Town J**					7 18		8 3				10 4		1116		1 5
216½	Wrafton					7 26		8 11				1015		1124		1 14
217½	Braunton **K**					7 31		8 16				1020		1128		1 19
223½	Mortehoe **L**					7 51		8 37				1039		1146		1 38
226½	**ILFRACOMBE** arr			a.m		8 0		8 46	a.m			1048		1155	a.m	1 47
—	**Barnstaple Junc.** dep			6 55		7 25		Stop	8 14			10 5			1139	1 10
214¼	Fremington			7 0		7 30			8 19			1010			1135	1 15
218	Instow			7 8		7 40			8 26			1017			1142	1 22
220½	**Bideford N**			7 15		7 51			8 34			1023			1148	1 34
225¾	**Torrington 353** arr			7 30		8 5			8 47			1037			1150	1 45
—	**Okehampton** dep						6 37						9 56			
202¾	Maddaford Moor Halt **P**												10 8			
206½	Ashbury, for North Lew						7 6						1016			
210¼	Halwill **Q** 358 arr						7 17			a.m			1024			
—	Halwill dep						7 25			8 53			1037			
213½	Dunsland Cross						7 31			8 59			1045			
218¼	Holsworthy						7 39			9 8			1054			
223	Whitstone & Bridgerule						7 48			9 18			11 7			
228¾	**Bude** arr						7 58			9 28			1117			
—	Halwill dep						7 29						1028			
215½	Ashwater						7 41						1037			
219	Tower Hill						7 52	a.m					1044			
224	Launceston						8 3	8 34					1052			
228¼	Egloskerry							8 42					11 3			
231¾	Tresmeer							8 51					1111			
236¾	Otterham **T**							9 1					1121			
241¼	Camelford **U**							9 11					1130			
243¾	Delabole							9 19					1137			
247¾	Port Isaac Road							9 27					1144			
250¼	St. Kew Highway							9 32					1149			
254¾	**Wadebridge 358** arr							9 40					1156			
261	358 Bodmin arr							10 6					1 6			
260	**Padstow** arr							10 4					1210			

Miles	Station	16	17	18	19	20	21	22	23	24	25	26	27	28	29	30
—	**Yeoford** dep	1220													1st & 3rd class Pullman Cars only to Ilfracombe. Supplementary fees charged	
187¾	Bow	1230			2 10											
191	North Tawton	1237			2 16							3 21				
93¾	Sampford Courtenay	1244														
197¾	Okehampton arr	1253			2 29							3 34		4 25		
—	**Okehampton** dep	1256			2 31							3 36		4 27		**Mondays, Fridays and Saturdays** Runs until 27th October, 1947
204	Bridestowe	1 14										3 51				
207¼	Lydford	1 22										3 58				
208¾	Brentor	1 26		p.m								4 2	p.m.			
213¾	Tavistock **C**	1 37		2 0	2 58							4 11	4 25			
220½	Bere Alston 357	1 52		2 11	3 10								4 36			
223	Bere Ferrers	1 59		2 17									4 42			
225	Tamerton Foliot	2 4		2 22									4 46			
227½	St. Budeaux, for Saltash	2 9		2 27									4 51			
228¾	Ford (Devon)	2 16		2 31									4 58			
229¾	**Devonport D** arr	2 20		2 35	3 28							4 38	5 2	5 16		
230¼	**PLY-** North Rd. "	2 29		2 41	3 35							4 44	5 7	5 25		
234	**MOUTH** Friary "	2 40		2 52	3 47							4 55	5 17	5 36		
—	**Yeoford** dep			**Saturdays only**	Refreshment Car, London to Exeter	2 13							Stop	**Mondays, Fridays and Saturdays.** Runs until 27th October, 1947. 1st & 3rd class Pullman Cars only to Plymouth. Supplementary fees charged		
186	Copplestone					2 19										
187½	Morchard Road					2 23										
190	Lapford					2 28										
193¾	Eggesford **F**					2 35					3 14					
197¾	South Molton Road **G**					2 42										
200¾	Portsmouth Arms					2 48										
204¼	Umberleigh					2 55										
207¼	Chapelton					3 0										
211½	**Barnstaple Junc. H** arr					3 7					3 44				4 49	
	Barnstaple Junc. H dep					3 9					3 49				4 50	
212¼	**Barnstaple Town J**					3 13					3 54				4 54	
216½	Wrafton					3 21					4 2					
217½	Braunton **K**					3 25					4 7				5 5	
223½	Mortehoe **L**					3 43					4 27				5 24	
226½	**ILFRACOMBE** arr			Stop		3 52					4 36				5 33	
—	**Barnstaple Junc.** dep					3 15					4 0					4 56
214¼	Fremington					3 20					4 5					5 1
218	Instow					3 27					4 12					5 12
220½	**Bideford N**					3 33					4 18					5 18
225¾	**Torrington 353** arr		p.m			3 44					4 31		p.m			5 29
—	**Okehampton** dep		1 20										3 55		**Mondays, Fridays and Saturdays** Runs until 27th October, 1947	
202¾	Maddaford Moor Halt **P**		1 33										4 8			
206½	Ashbury, for North Lew		1 39										4 17			
210¼	Halwill **Q** 358 arr		1 46										4 27			
—	Halwill dep		1 47										4 33			
213½	Dunsland Cross		1 54										4 41			
218¼	Holsworthy		2 3										4 50			
223	Whitstone & Bridgerule		2 13										4 59			
228¾	**Bude** arr		2 25	p.m									5 9			
—	Halwill dep			1 53									4 29			
215½	Ashwater			2 0									4 37			
219	Tower Hill			2 7									4 44			
224	Launceston			2 15									4 52			
228¼	Egloskerry			**Saturdays only**									5 3			
231¾	Tresmeer												5 11			
236¾	Otterham **T**												5 21			
241¼	Camelford **U**												5 29			
243¾	Delabole												5 37			
247¾	Port Isaac Road												5 46			
250¼	St. Kew Highway												5 52			
254¾	**Wadebridge 358** arr												6 1			
261	358 Bodmin arr												6 30			
260	**Padstow** arr												6 21			

Public Time Table 6 October 1947. *Authors Collection.*